Chaplaincy

Chaplaincy

The Missional Frontier

Edited by
IAN S. MARKHAM
and ELIZABETH H. CLARKE

WIPF & STOCK · Eugene, Oregon

CHAPLAINCY
The Missional Frontier

Wipf & Stock
An Imprint of Wipf and Stock Publishers
199 W. 8th Ave., Suite 3
Eugene, OR 97401

www.wipfandstock.com

PAPERBACK ISBN: 979-8-3852-5823-9
HARDCOVER ISBN: 979-8-3852-5824-6
EBOOK ISBN: 979-8-3852-5825-3

VERSION NUMBER 02/26/26

Contents

Preface | vii

Acknowledgments | ix

Contributors | xi

1 Prison Chaplaincy: Championing Human Dignity Within Correctional Facilities | 1
PRATIK K. RAY

2 Creating Sacred Space: Prison Chaplaincy | 19
LEANOR ORTEGA TILL

3 The Mission Field of Hospital Chaplaincy | 29
MELINA DEZHBOD

4 Islamic Perspective on Elderly Care | 44
SYAZANA DURRANI

5 From the Valley to the Open Plain: Reflections on the Role of Executive Officer for Mission and Ministry at Saint Francis Ministries, a Faith-Based Child and Family Welfare Agency | 60
THE REVEREND ANDREW T. O'CONNOR

6 School Chaplaincy: A Seed Worth Planting | 72
THE REV. ELIZABETH REES

7 Moving Church into the World: Religious Education and Practice in Schools | 91
REVEREND DR. STEFANIE TAYLOR

8 British Military Chaplaincy | 107
GILES LEGOOD

9 Raising Vocations for Military Chaplaincy | 120
ANN RITONIA

Preface

IAN S. MARKHAM AND ELIZABETH CLARKE

CHAPLAINCY HAS BECOME ONE of the most vital and life-giving expressions of ministry today. At Virginia Theological Seminary, we have watched this vocation grow in both number and importance, no longer seen simply as an alternative to parish ministry but as a calling that stands at the very heart of Christian service. Parish ministry remains a cornerstone for many who seek theological education, yet more and more students are discerning vocations that lead them into hospitals, schools, correctional facilities, the military, eldercare settings, and countless other places where God's people long for care, presence, and hope. This is not merely a trend but a sign of the times: as our society grows more diverse and as the church learns new ways of inhabiting the public square, chaplains remind us that the gospel is always on the move, meeting people where they are. At VTS, we are committed to preparing leaders who can step into these spaces with confidence, compassion, and a deep sense of God's mission.

This book, *Chaplaincy: The Missional Frontier*, is both a guide and an invitation. It gathers a rich array of voices—Christian and interfaith, American and international, lay and ordained—who together paint a picture of chaplaincy as ministry on the front lines of human experience. These writers show us how chaplains step into pluralistic and sometimes difficult settings to offer care, bear witness, and accompany others through moments of trauma, moral struggle, institutional pressure, and profound transformation. Their stories take us into hospital rooms and prison yards, school chapels and eldercare facilities, military bases and family-services agencies. Each chapter invites us to see chaplaincy not only as specialized ministry but as a way of being present to the world with courage and tenderness.

The chapters that follow will help you explore this wide landscape. Pratik K. Ray opens with a reflection on prison chaplaincy, showing how chaplains uphold human dignity and nurture hope within the harsh realities of incarceration. Leanor Till offers a moving first-person account of creating sacred space in a women's prison, where presence and relationship become channels of grace. Melina Dezhbod writes about hospital chaplaincy as a place of holy encounter, where chaplains walk with patients, families, and staff at life's most sacred thresholds.

The interfaith dimension is deepened by Syazana Durrani's essay on the Islamic perspective on elderly care, which invites readers into a vision of honoring elders as a spiritual practice. Andrew T. O'Connor then takes us into the life of a large faith-based agency, showing how chaplaincy-style leadership brings prayer and hope to children and families in crisis. Elizabeth Rees reflects on school chaplaincy as a ministry of worship, teaching, and belonging, while Stefanie Taylor encourages us to see schools as fertile ground for nurturing faith in a generation increasingly distanced from church life. Giles Legood offers a compelling portrait of military chaplaincy in Britain, weaving together its history and present challenges, and Ann Ritonia closes the volume with a heartfelt call to raise up new vocations for military chaplaincy, inviting the church to bless and support those called to serve in this demanding ministry.

Taken together, these essays remind us that chaplaincy is a place where God's Spirit is at work in powerful and surprising ways. Here we see the church moving out into the world—into places of suffering and joy, complexity and hope—and finding Christ already present. For those discerning a call to ministry, for congregations eager to understand where the Spirit is leading, and for all who care about the future of the church, this book is an invitation to imagine how chaplaincy might open new paths of service and deepen our witness to God's love.

Acknowledgments

This book began as a conference held on April 8–9, 2024, and it is a joy to acknowledge those who helped make that gathering possible. We are deeply grateful to Taryn Habberley in the dean's office for her skillful coordination and to the catering team at Meriwether Godsey for their hospitality and care. Our thanks extend to all who participated in what became a rich and memorable conversation about the nature and demands of chaplaincy. We are also indebted to our commissioning editor, Robin Parry, whose guidance and encouragement helped bring this project to completion.

FROM IAN MARKHAM

I am especially grateful to the Board of Virginia Theological Seminary for giving me the space to host conferences like this one. These gatherings are life-giving for our community and remind me why I love the work we do together. I am also deeply thankful for my coeditor, Beth Clarke, whose energy, insight, and attention to detail shaped this book at every stage—she has been a true partner in this work. And most of all, I thank my wife, Lesley. She knows how much this calling means to me, and she graciously shares me with projects like this one. Lesley, I could not do this without you.

FROM ELIZABETH CLARKE

I am deeply grateful to Ian Markham for giving me the opportunity to collaborate on this project. The diversity and quality of opportunities available to students at Virginia Theological Seminary under Dean Markham's faithful leadership are immense, and I am endlessly inspired by the work the seminary does. I also want to thank my family: my parents, Bob and Marianne, and my brother's family, Tom, Megan, Lelia, and Sedona. Your love and support mean the world to me.

Contributors

The Rev. Dr. P. K. Ray is an Episcopal Priest with 25 years of experience in prison and military chaplaincy. He is canonically resident in the Episcopal Diocese of the Rio Grande.

Leanor Ortega Till resides in Denver with her two teens, husband and pets. She serves as Chaplain at the Denver Women's Correctional Facility where she leads Christian chapels playing hymns in a more "Johnny Cash" style and provides interfaith support to those imprisoned there. On another note, she is the saxophonist of Five Iron Frenzy, a ska-core band still actively performing.

The Rev. Melina Dezhbod is the Assistant Rector at Saint Elizabeth's Episcopal Church in Ridgewood NJ. She holds an MSW and MDiv and brings experience in parish ministry, hospice, and hospital chaplaincy. She is passionate about pastoral care and walking alongside others through life's sacred moments.

Syazana Durrani is a chaplain and Certified Educator Candidate in Clinical Pastoral Education (ACPE). She serves as Manager of Clinical Pastoral Education at Goodwin Living in Northern Virginia, supporting chaplain formation in elder care and healthcare settings, shaped by Islamic spirituality.

The Reverend Andrew O'Connor is the Executive Officer for Mission & Ministry at Saint Francis Ministries, a child and family welfare/wellbeing organization rooted in the tradition of the Episcopal Church since 1945. Prior to SFM, he served churches in California and Kansas. He and his family happily reside in Wichita, KS.

The Rev. Elizabeth Rees is the Senior Chaplain of St. Stephen's & St. Agnes Episcopal School in Alexandria, Virginia. Before discovering the joys of school chaplaincy, Elizabeth was a lawyer and judicial clerk and then a parish priest. She is also a certified spiritual director. She is married and has three teenage and young adult children, the best chaplain trainers around!

The Reverend Dr. Stefanie Taylor is the Head Chaplain of Holy Innocents' Episcopal School in Atlanta, Georgia. She is also the integration advisor for the Spirituality Mind Body Institute in the Teacher's College at Columbia University. Ordained a priest in 2011, Dr. Taylor is a graduate of The University of South Carolina. She earned her MDiv at The General Seminary and her DEdMin at Columbia Theological Seminary.

The Rt. Rev. Ann Ritonia is the Bishop Suffragan of Armed Forces and Federal Ministries for the Episcopal Church. She is the first woman to serve in this role. She served in the United States Marine Corps and Marine Corps Reserve as an enlisted Marine and commissioned officer. Additionally, she has pastored Episcopal churches in Virginia, Connecticut and Maryland.

The Venerable Dr Giles Legood is Chaplain-in-Chief of the UK's Royal Air Force. A Church of England priest, before serving as a military chaplain, he worked for over a decade as a university chaplain.

1

Prison Chaplaincy

Championing Human Dignity Within Correctional Facilities

PRATIK K. RAY

Prison chaplains fulfill many of the same roles as chaplains who serve in other contexts, such as the military and healthcare facilities. Among the numerous roles they fulfill, they make rounds, provide pastoral care and counseling, lead worship services, teach classes, provide sacramental rites, participate in ceremonies, conduct morale and welfare events, advise on ethical issues, make death and illness notifications, and coordinate the accommodation of religious practices for all faith traditions. Prisons, jails, and detention centers, however, provide settings for ministry that are quite different from those in the free world, and some of the unique challenges within these environments are addressed in this paper.[1]

Prison housing units are designed based on the custody level of the imprisoned population, which is determined by several factors including an inmate's criminal history, past violent behavior, medical health, social background, special skills, affiliation with gangs or terrorist groups, and length of sentence. Classification levels and the labels used to describe them vary by jurisdiction (state and federal), but generally fit within the following groups. Maximum security provides the maximum level of control over inmates who are considered the most dangerous and disruptive. These persons are confined to a single occupancy cell and may be allowed

1. Ray, "Encountering."

out to utilize the law library or recreation area one hour a day, one inmate at a time, and under controlled movement. High and medium security facilities will typically house inmates in two- or three-person cells. During the day, these inmates are usually released from their cells and are free to move about the campus to use pay phones, spend time in the gym, go to the law library, take educational classes, and attend programs and services in the chapel. They also work at various jobs around the institution, preparing and serving food in the dining hall, doing laundry, mowing the lawn, and other tasks that maintain the correctional facilities. Low security prison facilities operate similarly to medium and high security facilities, but housing units are usually dormitory-style that allow more freedom of movement than being locked in individual cells. Minimum security inmates are considered "out custody" and may be housed in dormitory-style housing within a prison camp located outside the walls of a prison complex. Minimum security inmates have the most freedom of movement and can serve on work details outside the walls of a prison.

A single correctional institution is usually organized as a prison complex that contains multiple facilities of different security levels and missions. In addition to having facilities designated by security levels, prisons may have a transfer center where inmates are housed temporarily while in transit from one institution to another. Due to the transient nature of these units, movement of inmates is usually more restrictive than for inmates in the main population. Prisons will also have special housing units designated for inmates serving time in disciplinary segregation from the main population. In disciplinary segregation, inmates are confined to their cells similar to a maximum security unit, but they will often share a two-person cell.

Chaplains serving inside correctional institutions are granted unique access and influence to effect positive changes within the prison climate. As fully vetted employees of correctional facilities, prison chaplains carry the same status as the officers and can freely visit any areas of a prison complex with little or no restrictions on access. They therefore have a much greater ability to interact with and minister to incarcerated persons than visiting clergy from the outside. Further, like other correctional staff, chaplains have the same obligation to respond to emergencies (like fights on the recreation yard) and assist in restoring the safety and order of the prison. Because prison chaplains hold the status of being correctional workers, they possess a unique rapport and camaraderie with the staff of correctional institutions.

Within the confines of prisons of all security levels, prison chaplains must be prepared to minister to incarcerated women and men who are experiencing separation from family members and other support networks that they may have had on the outside. Additionally, these men and women may be experiencing shame and guilt from their loss of status and the stigmatization of being a convict. They may also be experiencing depression, loneliness, and hopelessness due to their loss of freedom and lack of control over their lives. As Winston Churchill famously stated:

> We must not forget that when every material improvement has been effected in prisons, when the temperature has been rightly adjusted, when the proper food to maintain health and strength has been given, when the doctors, chaplains, and prison visitors have come and gone, the convict stands deprived of everything that a free man calls life.[2]

Given these conditions, prisons offer a wealth of ministry opportunities.

Additionally, the dehumanization of prisoners and the apathy of some staff members towards prisoners inside prisons within the United States create additional challenges that prison chaplains must address. With more than two million prisoners, the United States leads the world in both the overall number of persons it incarcerates and in the percentage of its population that it incarcerates.[3] Within this context of mass incarceration, apathy, indifference, dehumanization, and substandard living conditions are well documented.

One example is a 2022 investigation of the Mississippi State Penitentiary Parchman in which the Civil Rights Division of the US Department of Justice found that the Mississippi Department of Corrections maintained a severely inhumane environment, stating, "The problems at Parchman are severe, systemic, and exacerbated by serious deficiencies in staffing and supervision" and that "[Mississippi Department of Corrections] has been on notice of these deficiencies for years and failed to take reasonable measures to address the violations."[4] The report describes how "deliberate indifference" caused "serious harm and a substantial risk of serious harm" to the prisoner population, citing, as an example, the conditions leading to a prison riot that began on December 31, 2019:

2. United Kingdom, Parliamentary Debates (Hansard), House of Commons, July 20, 1910, col. 1354 (Statement by the Rt. Hon. Winston S. Churchill).

3. Fair and Walmsley, "World."

4. US Department of Justice, "Investigation," 3.

> In the months leading up to the riot, there had been widespread reports about unlivable and unsanitary conditions throughout Parchman; violent murders and suicides on the rise; staffing plummeting to dangerous levels; and mounting concerns that gangs were filling the void left by inadequate staff presence and gaining increasing control of Parchman through extortion and violence.[5]

Among the deficiencies listed, the Department of Justice found that the Mississippi Department of Corrections "fails to protect incarcerated persons from violence at the hands of other incarcerated persons," noting the failures to provide adequate supervision, investigate serious incidents of harm, control dangerous contraband, control gang activity, and prevent extortion. Additionally, while the findings reported were limited to Parchman, the Department of Justice noted that it was still conducting investigations into three other Mississippi facilities.[6]

Another example is a limited-scope review of the Federal Bureau of Prisons' strategies to identify, communicate, and remedy operational issues, conducted in 2023 due to long-standing agency-wide issues. At one facility that had thirteen inmate suicides between 2012 and 2021, a consistent climate of indifference was noted:

> Between 2012 and 2021, 13 inmates have died by suicide at USP Atlanta, and five of those deaths occurred between October 2019 and June 2021. Past reconstruction teams have made many of the same recommendations noted below in this report: the need for attention to detail, adherence to BOP policy, and regard for human life among Correctional Services staff and, at times, other departments. Once again, this reconstruction revealed complacency, indifference, inattentiveness, and lack of compliance with BOP policies and procedures. These lapses contribute to a dangerous and chaotic environment of hopelessness and helplessness, leaving inmates to their own means to improve their quality of life.[7]

There are copious other examples that serve to demonstrate the scope of the problem of indifference and lack of regard for human life and human dignity in prison settings. Citing additional examples, however, is unnecessary since these conditions are so commonly known to the public, addressed by the media, and portrayed in movies and television shows. Given the

5. US Department of Justice, "Investigation," 3.
6. US Department of Justice, "Investigation," 4.
7. US Department of Justice, "Limited-Scope," 13.

pervasive inhumanity found within the prison walls of the United States, there is certainly much work that needs to be done in reforming prisons and the culture of mass incarceration. Prison chaplains can also do a lot of work in their local settings.[8]

These observations are not a judgment on the brave men and women who serve as correctional officers. I believe that most correctional workers have positive motivations for working in prisons, but that the climate created by mass incarceration greatly contributes to how staff members manage prison populations. This climate is shaped by the lack of adequate staffing, overcrowding, and lack of resources available for the inmate population. For example, the Department of Justice investigation of Parchman revealed that the lack of staffing creates an "authority vacuum" in which prisoners rather than staff control the units and where staff sometimes do not feel safe to respond to incidents and therefore "turn their backs" to incidents of violence.[9] In such an environment, apathy and indifference may function as necessary survival strategies for the staff who rely on their employment. These correctional officers may feel as powerless to address systemic and structural issues as the women and men in custody, so they prioritize their own wellbeing and safety.

CHAPLAINS AS CHAMPIONS OF HUMAN DIGNITY BEHIND PRISON WALLS

In response to the ubiquity of apathy and dehumanization within correctional institutions, prison chaplains are called to be on the forefront of the effort to counteract these negative attitudes. In their roles as institutional chaplains, they are not directly involved in making systemic changes to reform the prison industrial complex. They are, however, engaged in the equally important task of ministering to the incarcerated women and men housed within prisons. By showing up and impacting the life of even one incarcerated man or woman by a gesture or action that honors their human dignity, chaplains can make small differences that can have a ripple effect within their institutions. Little things like making rounds and asking inmates about their day and offering brief prayers or words of encouragement can build connections and foster hope. This ministry can be likened to the commonly shared illustration of a man walking along a beach who

8. US Department of Justice, "Investigation."

9. US Department of Justice, "Limited-Scope."

is observed picking up stranded starfish and throwing them back into the ocean. When questioned about how his actions could possibly make a difference, he replies (while tossing the next starfish back), "I made a difference to that one!"

Chaplains serving inside correctional institutions not only have unique access to effect positive changes inside these institutions, they are also uniquely called and appointed to do so. As ordained clergy, they are perceived as the religious leaders and God's representatives within prisons. They are the prophets who point to and embody a different way of living within the world behind bars. Given this role, they must serve as champions of hope and humanization who encourage and inspire others to recognize a deeper reality and a truer narrative than the narrative of apathy and indifference. The greater narrative that prison chaplains are called to share is the recognition of the profound value and inherent dignity of each and every human life jailed within the walls of correctional facilities. As ambassadors of God, chaplains must be the proclaimers of this good news to the imprisoned and their custodians.

The great majority of prison chaplains in the United States are Christian. In state prisons, as reported in a 2012 study, 71 percent of the chaplains identified as Protestant and an additional 13 percent identified as Catholic. Of the remaining non-Christian chaplains, 7 percent of state prison chaplains were Muslim and 3 percent were Jewish.[10] In the federal prison system, as reported in a 2021 audit, over 90 percent of the chaplains were Christian, with 84 percent identifying as Protestant. Of the 236 chaplains employed across 122 institutions, 199 were Protestant, 15 were Catholic, and 2 were Orthodox. Of the remaining non-Christian chaplains, 13 were Muslim, 4 were Jewish, 2 were Buddhist, and 1 was Messianic.[11]

In regard to the prison populations which they serve, state prison chaplains reported that Christians composed two-thirds of the incarcerated population, with "Protestants . . . comprising 51 percent of the inmate population, Catholics 15 percent and other Christian groups less than 2 percent."[12] In the federal prison system, Christians also compose about two-thirds of the inmate population. Of 118,330 inmates with documented religious affiliations, there were 40,797 Protestants, 29,553 Catholics, and an additional 4,649 representing other Christian groups. Non-Christian

10. Boddie and Funk, "Religion," 27.

11. US Department of Justice, "Limited-Scope," 1–3.

12. Boddie and Funk, "Religion," 23.

populations with more than 3,000 members included 11,073 Muslims, 5,743 Native Americans, 4,463 pagans, 3,455 practitioners of Santeria, 3,387 Rastafarians, and 3,298 Jews.[13]

BIBLICAL AND THEOLOGICAL FOUNDATIONS OF CHAMPIONING HUMAN DIGNITY

In championing the value and inherent dignity of the men and women in prison, the Christian understanding of humans as created in the image of God is a powerful focal lens through which prison chaplains may view the women and men whom they serve. The primary passage of Scripture that informs this understanding is Gen 1:26–31. The passage declares that humans bear the image of God, are made in the likeness of God, and are given dominion over the earth. Given these realities, all human beings possess a fundamental and inherent dignity that comes with bearing the image of God. Further, this status remains intact even for people who are incarcerated.

Archbishop Desmond M. Tutu eloquently and emphatically states this case in the following example:

> The life of every human person is inviolable as a gift from God. And since this person is created in the image of God and is a God carrier, a second consequence would be that we should not just respect such a person but that we should have a deep reverence for that person. The New Testament claims that the Christian person becomes a sanctuary, a temple of the Holy Spirit, someone who is indwelt by the most holy and blessed Trinity. We would want to assert this of all human beings. We should not just greet one another. We should strictly genuflect before such an august and precious creature. The Buddhist is correct in bowing profoundly before another human as the God in me acknowledges and greets the God in you. This preciousness, this infinite worth, is intrinsic to who we all are and is inalienable as a gift from God to be acknowledged as an inalienable right of all human persons. . . .
>
> All this makes human beings unique. It imbues each one of us with profound dignity and worth. As a result, to treat such persons as if they were less than this, to oppress them, to trample their dignity underfoot, is not just evil as it surely must be; it is not just painful as it frequently must be for the victims of injustice and

13. US Department of Defense, Office of the Inspector General, "Audit," 23.

> oppression. It is positively blasphemous, for it is tantamount to spitting in the face of God.[14]

While this passionate vision has been applied broadly to the struggles for human and civil rights, it is certainly applicable to prisoners and can serve to motivate prison chaplains in their approaches to ministry.

Additionally, what is called "the judgment of the nations" found in Matt 25:31–46 has been commonly interpreted to add an additional layer to this vision with specific reference to the prison ministry context. It equates visiting the prisoner with serving Christ, stating, "Just as you did it to one of the least of these brothers and sisters of mine, you did it to me."[15] This concept of the prisoner as "Christ in disguise" is a powerful image that can further inspire a prison chaplain's focus on human dignity as the chaplain sees Jesus in each of the faces of the incarcerated women and men that the chaplain serves.

Beyond seeing Jesus in the face of the prisoner, Jesus also serves as the exemplar for prison chaplains. Jesus's attitude can inform chaplains regarding what it means to recognize human value in the incarcerated women and men they serve even when those served may act out towards the chaplains in anger, disrespect, and violence. I shared this idea in one of my sermons when I proclaimed the following:

> Jesus serves as both icon and reality of the way of peace. He was hurt and wounded but did not return hurt for hurt or wound for wound. He takes the wound and does not excuse it, but he forgives it. He does not write off those offending persons, but instead reaches out with nail-scarred hands to bring those persons into healing and wholeness (back to their true selves because he sees their value, and their original goodness, and the image of God that is imprinted on their souls). They are too important, too precious, and too valuable to throw any of them away or write them off!
>
> Despite being injured, rejected, and hurt beyond comprehension, Jesus stayed true to himself (true to his full humanity and vulnerability) and to his vocation to redeem and restore the relationship. From the cross, he prayed, "Father, forgive them, for they do not know what they are doing." They are ignorant of their own dignity, their own worth, their own calling, and their own destiny with you. They are acting from a place of hurt, and fear, and anger, and hate, and blindness. They are acting out of their

14. Tutu, "First," 2.

15. Matt 25:40–41 NRSV.

> false self—their damaged self—not from the place of who they ultimately are . . . not from the place of what they were created to be, and what they are destined to be, and what they will be in you and by your design!
>
> Jesus recognized that underneath the angry, violent, bitter, and hateful person (even when acting against him) there was something beautiful, precious, and worth saving—that needed to be saved and needed to be restored![16]

Jesus recognized the original goodness and image of God even in those who acted murderously against him. His example is one that can encourage prison chaplains when they find themselves dealing with difficult or hostile prisoners. They may be inspired to share the Savior's attitude and similarly refuse to dismiss and write off inmates whose behaviors are violent or obscene toward the chaplains and other staff.

CHAMPIONING HUMAN DIGNITY IN CONGREGATIONAL WORSHIP

As worship leaders and preachers, prison chaplains can directly share a message of human dignity with their prison congregations in their teaching and preaching. Additionally, in conducting the sacramental liturgies of the church, prison chaplains may serve a particularly significant role in fostering human dignity as they invite incarcerated men and women into new identities as children of God and sisters and brothers in Christ.

In the Eucharist, the dignity of all participants is affirmed as "a new community is created that should endeavor to seek reconciliation among its members and with the wider world."[17] Further, the Eucharist "offers a foretaste of God's reign in which everyone is welcomed to Christ's table, especially those who are excluded from society."[18] Each participant may approach the table only because of God's grace. No one earns a place by their own merits, yet each is invited because of God's love. Also, by its communal nature, each participant becomes part of one family—sisters and brothers at one table together. Thus, the staff members and incarcerated men and women participating in the service are invited into a sacred space in which their identities as "officer" and "inmate" are subsumed into their greater

16. Ray, untitled and unpublished sermon, December 26, 2021.
17. Levad, *Redeeming*, 96.
18. Levad, *Redeeming*, 97.

identities as children of God and sisters and brothers in Christ. Additionally, in worship services that omit communion, participants still engage this reality as they corporately come together in prayer.

The physical human contact that takes place between prison chaplains and incarcerated men and women at congregational services and during specific sacramental rites takes on a heightened role of significance within the prison ministry context. This is because the only physical contact between staff members and incarcerated individuals that typically occurs happens when a person in custody is being pat searched, or handcuffed, or being escorted in chains. There is no authorized staff to inmate contact outside of these types of scenarios other than when an incarcerated person may be receiving medical or dental care. An exception to this practice is when a chaplain is providing services. For example, while prisoners and staff generally do not shake hands, chaplains will often shake hands with congregation members as they arrive or depart worship services. This may also happen during worship where there is a passing of the peace. Thus, the chapel becomes a thin space where the prison population and chaplains transcend their identities as inmates and staff and become brothers and sisters in Christ.

These encounters can be profoundly humanizing. Whereas most correctional staff only ever lay hands on prisoners to restrain, control, and inspect, chaplains lay their hands on prisoners to bless, heal, and comfort. For example, in a maximum security unit where inmates remain locked in their cells, chaplains may offer the rite of anointing with oil (or impose ashes on Ash Wednesday). In these instances, a chaplain would ask an officer to open the food slot in the prisoner's cell door (which is designed to pass food trays in and out of the cell). The prisoner could kneel or bend down and present his or her forehead near the slot opening through which the chaplain would make the sign of the cross on his or her forehead. Whereas these rites mediate certain meanings within their liturgical and theological contexts, the very act of the chaplain touching the forehead of the prisoner communicates that she or he has dignity and is worthy of being touched. Another example is the experience of a chaplain who conducted a Maundy Thursday foot washing service in a prison chapel. He shared that as he began to wash one incarcerated man's feet, the man began to tremble and his eyes started to tear. The man said, "Chaplain, this is the first time that someone has touched me in twenty years!"

CHAMPIONING HUMAN DIGNITY IN FACILITATING FOR ALL RELIGIOUS TRADITIONS

While the great majority of prison chaplains are Christian clergy serving incarcerated populations whose majority identify as Christian, prison chaplains spend significant amounts of time in accommodating a wide variety of congregational services. Chaplains coordinate the use of chapel spaces, multipurpose rooms, and outdoor worship areas to host various meetings. For example, chaplains may coordinate the main indoor worship space to be set up with prayer rugs on Friday afternoons to host Muslim Jum'ah prayer services and then have it set up with chairs and a communion table on Sundays to host Christian services. Prison chaplains will also open the chapel on Friday evenings and Saturday mornings for Jewish prisoners and others who observe Sabbath worship. They may also have to supervise incarcerated persons worshiping outdoors, such as a Native American sweat lodge ceremony or an Odinist or Wiccan ritual.

In order to support the various faith groups for which prison chaplains cannot directly provide, chaplaincy departments work closely with the religious groups and agencies in their local communities to identify and recruit volunteer clergy and lay representatives. Prison chaplains spend time vetting and training these representatives. Also, once the volunteers are cleared to enter, chaplains spend time escorting them in and out of the prisons, monitoring their activities, and monitoring and supervising inmates that participate in the volunteer-led services. Depending on the facility, some volunteers obtain "unescorted" credentials that allow them to enter and leave the facility without needing the constant supervision of a prison chaplain. In these situations, prison chaplains still provide intermittent supervision and are responsible for oversight of the volunteers' activities. Additionally, chaplaincy departments will sometimes contract for a paid religious provider to lead services for a specific faith group when no chaplain or volunteer provider is available.

When there are no chaplains, volunteers, or contractors available to lead congregational services within prisons, prisoners may still be allowed to meet as a group. These meetings are known as "inmate-led" services. These services are quite common and they provide particular challenges and responsibilities for prison chaplaincy staff. Prison policies and sound correctional practices prohibit the placing of individual inmates in positions of leadership over other inmates. Having "inmate-imams" or "inmate-preachers" who lead their congregations violates these policies. Prison chaplains must therefore proactively engage inmate religious groups to ensure that prisoners rotate responsibilities and speaking roles. Further, chaplains need to carefully monitor what inmates share and teach in these services. Prison chaplains may accomplish this by either being physically present at the service or through audiovisual surveillance equipment.

The logistical support prison chaplains provide in facilitating for congregational religious services is quite extensive. In supporting the Native American sweat lodge, prison chaplains purchase and maintain ceremonial tobacco, animal skulls, antlers, various herbs like sweet grass and sage, drums, firewood, rocks, and various tools and ceremonial items. They may have to coordinate receiving eagle feathers from the National Eagle Repository through the US Fish and Wildlife Service for an inmate with documented membership in a tribe. For practitioners of Santeria and other orisha worshipers, chaplains may provide coconuts, egg shell powder, candles, incense, drums, bells, sea shells, statues, and images of the orishas, along with many other possible ceremonial items. They also carefully maintain and ration out small cigars for use in orisha worship. Additionally, there are many other faith groups that prison chaplains support, and the range and variety of items that chaplains purchase and maintain for these groups may be similarly extensive.

Prison chaplains play a large role in coordinating and supporting the annual religious holidays of all faith traditions. For example, during Ramadan, chaplains will adjust their schedules in order to have the chapel open every evening of the month in order for Muslim inmates to pray together after sunset and before breaking their fasts for that day. In preparation for the Jewish Passover, prison chaplains survey the inmate population several weeks ahead of the holiday to determine who will need kosher for Passover meals. They then coordinate with their food services departments to ensure special food trays are provided to participating inmates throughout the eight days of this holiday. They may also coordinate having special kosher for Passover snacks available for purchase at prison commissaries during this time. Before the festival of Sukkot, prison chaplains work with Jewish inmates to construct temporary shelters that meet their religious requirements while not violating the safety and security of the prison. Then, during the days of the festival, prison chaplains coordinate the movement of prisoners so that they can utilize the shelters.

In addition to facilitating congregational services, prison chaplains must be available to assist each inmate as individual practitioners of their various religious traditions. For example, if inmates have specific religious dietary needs, they may have to be interviewed and approved by a chaplain before being placed on a list to receive kosher- or halal-certified food trays. Prisoners usually also have to go through the chaplains in order to purchase individually owned religious property. Religious property includes headwear such as turbans, crowns, hijabs, scarfs, kufis, yarmulkes, and bandanas. It also includes items like religious necklaces, prayer rugs, tarot cards, prayer beads, and religious undergarments.

For prisoners in housing units that remain locked down, prison chaplains make rounds and distribute copies of sacred texts and donated religious magazines. As requested by the prisoners, prison chaplains may pray at the door with the inmates and provide any appropriate religious rites according to their religious organizations. Chaplains may also escort volunteers and contract religious providers of various faith traditions to visit inmates in these housing units so that they can pray with the inmates and provide appropriate rites and sacraments from their traditions. Chaplains may also distribute items for inmates to perform their own rituals, such as delivering grape juice and matzo crackers to Jewish inmates on Friday afternoons before the Sabbath in order for them to recite the kiddush with their evening meal.

From a Christian perspective, the work of serving and accommodating practitioners of all faiths can be viewed as holy work. Without proselytizing, prison chaplains are able to share their faith incarnationally through these many acts of service to the inmate population. By respecting religious freedom and impartially accommodating all, prison chaplains demonstrate graciousness, hospitality, and acceptance. This models and embodies the self-giving love that is so central to the Christian faith. Additionally, as prison chaplains learn about other traditions and interact with other faith communities, they build relationships of mutual respect and understanding that can contribute to interfaith cooperation. In dispelling stereotypes and overcoming prejudices, these relationships foster the honoring of the human dignity in all people.

CHAMPIONING HUMAN DIGNITY IN NON-FAITH GROUP SPECIFIC TRAINING

Beyond providing for the religious needs of inmates, prison chaplains facilitate classes directed at the self-improvement and rehabilitation of prisoners in order to enhance their lives while incarcerated and prepare them for re-entry into the community. These are offered to the entire inmate population. Since these classes are offered under the auspices of the chapel, they may include faith-based elements or focus on spiritual resilience. When this is the case, these classes can facilitate powerful peer learning as incarcerated persons share the wisdom and practices from religious traditions that they have practiced and from their personal experiences. Additionally, some individuals come to prison having had little to no interaction with people of other races, cultures, religions, values, and worldviews. Participating in these chapel programs can greatly increase their exposure to other ways of thinking and may somewhat resemble the experience of a person who goes away to college and receives a liberal arts education.

One class that chaplains facilitate in several prisons is based on the book *Houses of Healing: A Prisoner's Guide to Inner Power and Freedom*. Without delving into the doctrines of any particular religion, the author teaches the foundational idea that participants must recognize their "core Self" which could also be described as their "free Self, greater Self, true Self, or essential Self."[19] She shares that each person is born with "a core of awareness and creative will whose job it is to help us fulfill our true nature, to become truly confident, loving, caring, and wise."[20] This true Self, however, gets overlaid and hidden underneath "small selves" and "sub-personalities" that emerge during the difficulties and traumas of living.[21] As the course progresses and participants work through the exercises in the book, the spiritual journey they make very much parallels the Christians' journey of discovering that buried and hidden underneath sin, ignorance, and people's false ideas about themselves is the profound reality of their value, dignity, and goodness as bearers of the image of God. This spiritual journey also has parallels in many of the other great religious traditions of the world. The *Houses of Healing* course serves as a great example of how prison chaplains

19. Casarjian, *Houses*, 11.
20. Casarjian, *Houses*, 11.
21. Casarjian, *Houses*, 13–14.

can champion human dignity through the lens of humans made in the image of God in a manner that does not proselytize or indoctrinate.[22]

CHALLENGES TO PRISON CHAPLAINCY

There are many unique challenges to serving as prison chaplains. Prison chaplains have to maintain the strictest boundaries regarding even the smallest requests to ensure that they accommodate requests fairly. This is to ensure that they uphold the commonly quoted trio of principles of being "firm, fair, and consistent." This is also often stated as "What you do for one, you must do for all." If prison chaplains fail to maintain these boundaries, they will find themselves inadvertently establishing precedents that they and other chaplains may have to enforce. These may even carry over into other correctional institutions. Sometimes, new religious property items or congregational religious practices will emerge that should be recognized and accommodated, but these should be carefully evaluated in consultation with a prison agency's chaplaincy branch leadership.

One example is religious headwear. Several types of religious headwear are already approved to be worn in most prisons. In the Federal Bureau of Prisons, the following headwear is authorized for male inmates to wear throughout the institutions: black or white yarmulkes, black or white kufis, white turbans, black crowns (with red, yellow, and green stripes), and multicolored headbands. If a male inmate asserts that these items do not meet the needs of his religious group and that he needs to be authorized to wear a blue kufi, a prison chaplain cannot simply grant the request. If the chaplain does this, that chaplain has just inadvertently added to the list of authorized items for the prison. Also, if one inmate is granted the right to wear a blue kufi, then this right must be extended to others. Additionally, when inmates with blue kufis transfer to other facilities, it would be hard for those facilities to deny them the right to wear these because they can say, "The chaplain at my last institution let me have this. Why is it not authorized here?"

In the blue kufi example, there are also further considerations. In introducing new and unfamiliar practices or religious items, if the threshold for approval is impossibly high, then legitimate religious needs may be unduly curtailed. However, if the threshold for approval is low and easily met, one could see how quickly the amounts and kinds of approved religious

22. Casarjian, *Houses*.

items could increase and become unmanageable. For example, other colors of headwear and other types of headwear might quickly be introduced. If the threshold for approval is low enough, inmates could easily go beyond headwear and initiate requests for various types and colors of religious footwear. And this could go on and on, overwhelming the system.

Prison chaplains must intentionally and critically exercise boundaries for all kinds of requests that would not likely be an issue outside the prison context. For example, a prisoner may state that they need to mail a legal document right away, but they cannot make copies in the law library because its copier is down. They may ask the chaplain if they can make a quick copy on the chapel copier. This may seem like a harmless and simple request, but if the chaplain grants the request, then the chaplain should be prepared to allow everyone else in the inmate population to have a turn to make copies on the chapel copier. Otherwise, the chaplain is not being "firm, fair, and consistent" and could be accused of giving special favors to some inmates and not others. Also, when chaplains grant such requests once, they should be prepared to have inmates expect the favor to be granted again and again. They may say, "You let me make copies last week. Why can't you help me this week?"

Favors can also be a slippery slope towards compromising a prison chaplain. An inmate may say, "I won't tell anyone you let me make copies last week, but can you please give me a phone call today?" The implied threat is that the inmate will report the chaplain's previous behavior unless the chaplain agrees to the next favor. However, granting the next favor will simply lead to greater compromises. For example, the inmate may then come back with, "I am not going to say anything about the phone call you let me have last week, but I do need you to bring in a pack of cigarettes for me. My family will Venmo you the money to pay for it."

Prison chaplains also need to maintain strict boundaries when conducting door-to-door rounds in transfer centers and special housing units. When walking a range, chaplains might announce themselves: "Chaplain on the range!" As they travel from one cell door to the next, the inmates in the surrounding cells are usually listening intently to the chaplains' conversations. Since, for security reasons, inmates in transfer centers are usually transported to the in-transit location without prior notice, an inmate might say, "Would you please give me a phone call? My family doesn't know that I'm here, and I need to check on my mom, who is sick." If a chaplain grants the request and has the inmate pulled from his cell to make a phone call, all the other prisoners on the range that witnessed the encounter will be ready to make a similar request and will be prepared to loudly protest if not given the same treatment as the first inmate.

If a chaplain does not grant the request, the inmate may make a follow-on request, such as, "Well, could you at least call my family and let them know that I will be here for a few days?" If a chaplain agrees to this request, they will be leaving the transfer center with a list of two hundred calls that they agreed to make, one for each inmate on the unit. Additionally, each call would lead to family members asking questions about their incarcerated loved ones and wanting the chaplains to deliver messages back to the inmates. Prison chaplains must therefore decline these types of requests. There are circumstances where prison chaplains do assist in providing special phone calls for inmates, such as when there is a verified death or hospitalization of an immediate family member or close relative, but the criteria chaplains use must be strictly adhered to in order to prevent being overwhelmed.

Making rounds and providing door-to-door ministry for inmates who are locked down is challenging. One can only imagine how boring and depressing it must be for incarcerated persons in these types of units, just waiting and looking out the narrow window in their cell doors. Therefore, a prison chaplain's visit may provide significant encouragement and the donated literature that the chaplain delivers may serve as a valuable resource in passing the time. Some inmates, however, might find it entertaining to mock and harass the chaplain. They might start yelling and stirring up other inmates on the unit who may also engage in the taunting for lack of anything else more entertaining to do in the moment.

Prison chaplains, therefore, need to be thick-skinned and sure of their callings. They will not do well if they need constant encouragement and positive feedback from those they serve. They also need to be confident in their judgments regarding religious accommodations and not feel bad when they must refuse requests. This can be hard for chaplains since many clergy members have a strong emotional need to please others. While it is healthy for prison chaplains to experience personal satisfaction in providing ministry, they cannot rely on the inmate population to meet their emotional needs. It is vital that prison chaplains remain self-aware. It is also important for prison chaplains to tend to their overall wellness outside of work. Having a counselor, spiritual director, or other trusted confidant with whom they can verbally process the encounters that they have had inside the prison is also helpful. If prison chaplains ignore self-care, they put themselves in danger of violating their boundaries and becoming compromised.

BIBLIOGRAPHY

Boddie, Stephanie C., and Cary Funk. "Religion in Prisons: A 50-State Survey of Prison Chaplains." Pew Research Center Forum on Religion and Public Life, March 22, 2012. https://www.pewresearch.org/wp-content/uploads/sites/7/2012/03/Religion-in-Prisons.pdf

Casarjian, Robin. *Houses of Healing: A Prisoner's Guide to Inner Power and Freedom.* Dedham, MA: Lionheart, 1995.

Fair, Helen, and Roy Walmsley. "World Prison Population List." Institute for Crime and Justice Policy Research, 2021. https://www.prisonstudies.org/sites/default/files/resources/downloads/world_prison_population_list_13th_edition.pdf.

Levad, Amy. *Redeeming a Prison Society: A Liturgical and Sacramental Response to Mass Incarceration.* Minneapolis: Fortress, 2014.

Ray, Pratik. "Encountering the Imago Dei in Ministry with the Incarcerated." DMin thesis, Wesley Theological Seminary, 2024.

Tutu, Desmond. "The First Word: To Be Human Is to Be Free." In *Christianity and Human Rights: An Introduction*, edited by John Witte Jr. and Frank S. Alexander, 1–7. Cambridge: Cambridge University, 2010.

United Kingdom, Parliamentary Debates (Hansard), House of Commons, July 20, 2023. https://api.parliament.uk/historic-hansard/commons/1910/jul/20/class-iii.

US Conference of Catholic Bishops. "The Corporal Works of Mercy." https://www.usccb.org/beliefs-and-teachings/how-we-teach/new-evangelization/jubilee-of-mercy/the-corporal-works-of-mercy.

US Department of Justice, Civil Rights Division. "Investigation of the Mississippi State Penitentiary (Parchman)." April 20, 2022. https://www.justice.gov/opa/press-release/file/1495796/download.

US Department of Justice, Federal Bureau of Prisons. "Religious Beliefs and Practices." October 24, 2022. https://www.bop.gov/policy/progstat/5360_010_cn.pdf.

US Department of Justice, Office of the Inspector General. "Audit of the Federal Bureau of Prisons' Management and Oversight of its Chaplaincy Services Program." July 7, 2021. https://oig.justice.gov/sites/default/files/reports/21-091.pdf.

———. "Limited-Scope Review of the Federal Bureau of Prisons' Strategies to Identify, Communicate, and Remedy Operational Issues." May 2023. https://oig.justice.gov/sites/default/files/reports/23-065.pdf.

2

Creating Sacred Space

Prison Chaplaincy

LEANOR ORTEGA TILL

It's lockdown at the prison.

ALL OFFENDERS AT DENVER Women's Correctional Facility have fifteen minutes to quickly make their way to their own cell to be counted in. This was not a scheduled count, so I have made my way with my acoustic child-sized guitar to unit 2, and I have been setting up for chapel. It's a typical winter Tuesday. Normally, this large unit's main room would have ladies working quietly on puzzles and be filled with the smells of Doritos, beans, popcorn, and other snacks coming from the microwave. Normally, the TV would be playing an action movie too loud for my taste. Normally there would be a puppy or two in training that I would be encouraged to pet. But not today. As the offenders make their way, I am looking at my empty chairs with sets of multicolored paper on them. Each chair has a handful of the old greats, as I think of them. "Old Rugged Cross," "Just a Closer Walk with Thee," the old hymns our golden-year ladies might recognize as well as the newer K-Love hits, "10,000 Reasons," "My Chains are Gone." What to do? I already drove forty-five minutes to the prison. I already passed through a series of metal detectors, secured vestibules surrounded by barbed wire fences and video cameras, and made my way across the yard to be here. Too late to go back. My child-sized acoustic classical guitar fits perfectly in my small hands. I begin to strum "Amazing Grace." I have never heard this space, concrete cinder block, so hushed. It's almost sacred and about to become more so as my voice fills the void. "Amazing grace, how sweet the sound . . ." What must the correctional officers think? I don't care, knowing that I can stop singing as quickly as I began. And just like that I am in a chapel, a house of worship. I find it kind of funny that even the ladies who would normally keep their distance from the chaplain are able to hear these songs and *not* able to go anywhere else to not hear them. It's a typical day in the prison, meaning not typical at all.

MY UNCONVENTIONAL JOURNEY TO PRISON MINISTRY

I'm a spirit-led speaker and creative servant, passionately sharing the life-changing love of Christ. My path to this point has been anything but ordinary. At eighteen, in an act of radical faith that eluded my traditional Mexican-American parents, I left college to travel the world, touring in a school bus to play saxophone in the Christian ska punk band Five Iron Frenzy. Over the course of the nine years in which we toured the US and abroad, I grew fiercely committed to serving all of Christ's community, from the misfits and skeptics to the earnest and eager believers.

With a loud laugh, high energy level, and heart for encouragement, I love teaching Christ's word, mostly using current slang and visual metaphors! So many people don't fit into the church stereotype. The core of my ministry is to cultivate loving and encouraging communities that honor the dignity of the human spirit in sometimes difficult situations.

All over the world God is building church in surprising places, and we will be the most surprised if we join in this movement! The life of a chaplain engages a broader audience than I ever had faith to dream, and the impact made on the prison culture is powerful.

After obtaining a bachelor's degree in sociology with a minor in Spanish, I settled back into my Colorado punk community and became integrally involved in the church born out of our band's Bible study, Scum of the Earth Church. Scum was birthed in 2000 and was the incubator for my early ministry. The richness of the relationships that I've made in my community of faith, spanning time and place, was awe-inspiring and led me to my current calling as a pastor who serves beyond the church's walls with a passion to reach those who might never step foot inside its doors.

IN THE BEGINNING

I began my relationship with prison ministry in the way most people must, meaning it had never crossed my mind when someone out of the blue suggested it. While visiting a "pay-what-you-can" cafe with my two- and four-year-olds, a volunteer employee began to talk with me. She learned I was on staff at Scum of the Earth Church in downtown Denver and suggested I join her in prison ministry. Pat explained that most of the volunteers were of retirement age and that they really were hoping to get more ladies in their thirties, like me. Of course, being in my thirties meant I had no time to commit, but I did take her phone number and promised to call her when my situation changed. True to my word, seven years later, I called her!

"Pat! Do you remember me? It's Leanor, from Scum. Now that my kids are older, I can get involved in the prison."

"Great, we are having an event next weekend."

GROWING PAINS

Kairos Prison Ministry is a well-known and large organization serving both men's and women's prisons. Kairos programs and the training manuals are extensive and rarely veer from the courses set. I appreciate my time growing and learning in this group. The main mantra we stick to is "*Listen listen love love*." Now that caught my attention! But the problem is I am a talker! I am known for being very high energy, a bit direct, loud, impatient, and outspoken, and a typical eight on the Enneagram! "*Listen listen*" was going to be a challenge! Fortunately I found mentors in women that were completely blessed in the listening department and very soon I found myself latching onto and shadowing chaplain Tina, the resident, and eldest, of the group.

Chaplain Tina is a quiet person. She has a prison uniform but it's not typical. She wears a pale blue sweatshirt with embroidered chickadees and tan slacks. She has short unfussy hair and clear blue eyes. She is a saint in my mind. Her background was as an Episcopal priest but following a medical issue, she was unable to lead a congregation and found herself serving more at the women's prison. They adore her. It would take a very special person to fill her tiny shoes. I asked her if I may do so. After four years of shadowing her, she finally said yes!

I have asked my friends and family before to guess the phrase I hear the most when I am walking across the Yard. Educated by TV shows and movies, most of them guess things like, "F**k you," "Get out of my face," "I'm coming after you," etc. But nothing could be further from the truth. "I LOVE YOU!" Those three words enter my ears and touch my heart when I cross the Yard, and they are being yelled for all to hear! For those who live in units together in their small world, like a city, they become a family. Not allowed to hug or call one another on the phone, they instead shout their "I LOVE YOU"s loud and proud for all to hear! "I love you girl. You got this. I miss you Mija! Stay strong sister!" The mantras of the yard.

DENVER WOMEN'S CORRECTIONAL FACILITY

After seven years of volunteering at the prison I began to find myself completely drawn in. Being a chaplain at a Level 4 prison demands a certain confidence and respect. Level 4 prisons are maximum security by design, created to rehabilitate and house the offenders that have committed what society might deem "the worst crimes," and who serve the longest sentences. This does not hinder the type of ministry we can host/create/engage in however. Because most of the offenders will be here decades and some for the remainder of their lives, there is a certain acceptance in the population. Cells become homes. Units become apartment buildings. Other offenders become closer than family members. Chaplains become pastors and religious programs become all they know of the church. It is what it is and it does bring a tremendous amount of peace and calm knowing what to expect day to day, unlike jail ministry, which tends to be chaotic and more stressful due to their transient and undiagnosed population.

Colorado State of Corrections's mission is to protect the citizens of Colorado by holding incarcerated persons accountable and engaging them in opportunities to make positive behavioral changes and become law-abiding, productive citizens.

Part of the challenge of serving in a Level 4 prison is that, since it is run by the State of Colorado, it has its own policies and procedures, hundreds of them! All of these are important for the safety of those who serve the prison and those imprisoned there. This means lots of training! All the volunteers serving at the Denver complex are vetted, trained, and closely overseen by the Faith and Citizens' program. I don't know if most correctional facilities have this type of program, but we are very blessed by ours.

Trained volunteers lead various programs, from the most traditional Bible studies to more creative spiritual programs such as yoga classes, meditation, and centering prayer. Therapeutic secular programs are also offered such as drum circles, art-based therapy, and behavior modification classes like anger management, AA, Cocaine Anonymous, etc. I began as a Christian faith-based volunteer through a program called Kairos Prison Ministry. Through the years I have learned that there were so many larger needs from the general population at DWCF. I began to long and pray for a larger role.

Understanding that chaplains are not financially state-supported, the Department of Corrections recognizes that a chaplain's absence from the facility for the purpose of raising financial support is necessary for the continued provision of chaplaincy services. I am entrusted with the mission to ask earnest and eager people to join my unconventional journey. Their prayers, encouragement, and financial support fuel the heart of my ministry.

SO WHAT DOES A PRISON CHAPLAIN DO?

When I am sitting on a plane minding my own business and my neighbor casually asks me, "What do you do?" and I say, "I'm a prison chaplain," eyes always widen. I imagine they want to ask me the same thing: "Do you know murderers?" I do. And I know convicted burglars, drug dealers, bank robbers, pedophiles, and dozens of other professional criminals too. The key to how I treat people is this very important protocol that I adhere to. I do not ask offenders what their crime was. Who does this protect?

Mainly me, if I am honest. What a gift to be able to see Angela as Angela and not a woman who attempted to murder someone. If offenders want to share their crime they occasionally will do so in the context of their story and hope for growth and redemption. It is always in the context of rehabilitation, not standalone statements merely said to impress me or scare me away. Personal information may run rampant in the system, but with respect and boundaries, chaplains are able to meet each person as they find them.

So what is the point of having a chaplain in the prison? This is a good question, especially considering the large majority of offenders there do not want to be in contact or relationship with one. We are there for the ones that want us, that need us even when they may not want us. First, it is our job to inform people when a loved one has passed away. This information comes best from us rather than a correctional officer because we represent care, concern, and do not represent authority and neutral or negative emotion. People are safe to be vulnerable with us. We provide professional pastoral care services for offenders, and department of corrections employees when requested, exercising pluralistic sensitivity to those of all faith backgrounds.

As chaplains, our job description is to provide: spiritual counseling; crisis intervention; grief counseling; in-person meetings with offenders in times of family medical emergency or to notify of a death of a loved one; acquiring and distributing faith-based materials; planning, developing, and implementing religious programs; and recruiting and coordinating volunteers for those programs. Finally, and I have yet to do this, but have high hopes for two offenders that have put in their papers, we may, as appropriate, maintain professional contact with post-release offenders, with approval of the Faith and Citizens Programs Administrator.

Inmates take a risk being hospitable, friendly, involved. They may be seen as hypocritical, weak, Goody Two-shoes, or brainwashed. In some ways, because of my affinity for punk rock culture and music, I get that. I too am someone who is suspicious of authority and wants to live against the grain. I too want to fully live rather than merely survive.

People with short sentences may want just that, to merely survive and therefore distract themselves. They are not interested in using their "free time" in programs that offer growth and consider their time in prison as something they need to make it through, a punishment, not a tool for rehabilitation.

PERSONAL REFLECTIONS

I am asked if I'm ever afraid, and I have never truly been fearful in the prison. There was a new, somewhat hyper-aware emotion I experienced when I first walked through the yard by myself. My lanyard with my keys would jingle and the reminder of all my years of training became front and center in my mind. I found myself taking longer and harder steps; some authority was showing through my movements even though I was barely trying. Here I was, a chaplain, with permission and a personal welcome from Warden Long to visit most places unaccompanied. After years in this role those emotions wore off and I didn't feel them again until I found myself walking through the yard at the male facility next-door. This was a much stronger feeling than I felt at the women's prison. My face began to flush and I was aware of male offenders turning toward me. Do I feel unsafe? No, but I know that I need to be aware and prepared for anything. I still feel this way at the DRDC but I have only been ministering there for two months as I write this.

Having keys in the prison is a game changer. The jingling of my keys and lanyard makes it obvious I belong there. It is easier and much quicker to get somewhere without going through mazes of stairwells. I can access the elevator to assist those in wheelchairs. I can open doors! But I was told if I lost my keys, I owe $5,000. I'm pretty sure that was a made-up number to scare me, but I am not taking any chances!

I took my photo for my official state ID in the exact same place inmates take their mug shots! In fact several newly arrested men were waiting to get their booking photograph taken and saw me, in "civilian" clothing, jump the line. They were asking me if I could get them a Bible. A curtain was then pulled down for my ID to cover the height chart placed on the concrete wall. It was all somewhat intimidating then but not now.

"Did you Pledge the Lord's guitar? You need to Pledge it!" Mechelle requested. Like an ordination for an instrument? Appointing it as a called instrument in service to the Lord? No. Literal Pledge, as in the furniture polish. She was sick of my sticky hand prints all over the varnish! Ha! When she finds it dirty she will use the bottom of her own sweatshirt to wipe it. Very humbling. Reminds me of the woman who used her hair to anoint Jesus's feet with perfume.

STORIES FROM THE INFIRMARY

After seven years of serving only at the women's prison chaplain Cathy had invited me to serve alongside her at the infirmary. This area houses both men and women that are in need of constant medical supervision. I have never been comfortable around those in medical pain, although any other pain I am fine with. I once fainted watching the nurses take blood from my Abuela, her weak arm looked so thin. Bam! I fainted and fell down to the concrete! For some reason, though, I have not felt any queasiness at the infirmary, although I have to say I struggle at the smell of ramen noodles Ms. Becker prepares with hot coffee instead of water!

I pass by the nurses' station first as always to see which people would definitely *not* want a visit from the chaplain and which new patients are in closed custody. The nurse says, "Would you visit Patterson in room 2? He is dying but he doesn't know it. We are just keeping him comfortable at this point." Wide-eyed but willing, I head down the hall to a very small and dark room with the door partly closed. It's always somewhat unsettling to see the visible steel toilet in the back of the room. Similarly, I have always found it shocking but fascinating that on the fronts of the doors of the infirmary are taped original mug shots of the offenders. Hardened faces and heads full of hair or beards are pictured, but it never reflects the person I am about to meet. This time Patterson is a small shell of a bald man attached to a large oxygen tank. After introducing myself I begin to sing "Silent Night" and other songs I used to sing to my kids while they were little. During "Amazing Grace" his body seems to relax, his eyeballs roll back gently, and he seems peaceful. Perhaps it is a terrible prayer, and Lord forgive me if it is, but I keep hoping he might peacefully pass away while I am there so he won't die alone.

Dak loved to read deep, theological books, ones that were required reading for those in seminary! It was hard to keep up with him; he was always ready for more books!

Weekly he received a small stack of books, and he would discuss them with us and offer his insights and opinions. As his understanding grew so did his prayers. As more bad news about his diagnosis and more intense medical treatments came, Dak vulnerably shared that, while he was not afraid to die, he was afraid to die alone. God answered the prayer!

Ms. Becker is a small lady, but no less fierce. She has sparkling blue eyes and a German accent. She is brilliant. It's painful to know that after thirty-two years in prison she has developed Parkinson's disease and has officially been granted medical parole. This means—*she can leave*. At eighty-three she has nowhere to go so she lives in the infirmary.

During Christmas I would sing for her. She requested "Danny Boy," and I promised to learn it. I thought it was a love song; I was so wrong. Opening YouTube to memorize the lyrics I found myself bawling to a song about death. Last week we sang it together. I look forward to seeing her on Fridays. She calls me a spitfire and "just a kid." I'm forty-seven years old!

Reese was feeling very upbeat and hopeful and came out to talk after receiving news that his daughter, who works for the state, on his behalf, reached out to a prominent TV lawyer. Is false hope a positive? Well, far be it from me to discourage it. His roomie was silently raising his eyebrows and very slightly shaking his head. No, I would never take a person's hope. Consider the Chinese culture; out of respect and love they choose to not tell others if they are sick for fear it would take the hope from living. This situation is similar. We do not take away hope when it might be all that they have.

IN-DEPTH ENCOUNTERS

LaVerne is a woman of personality. She stands out in a crowd because she has hair styled like a tough guy and tough-guy tattoos all over, but she also stands out because she is confident. The first time I met her was over a year ago when I started in prison ministry. She attended a four-day intensive event and the first thing she said to me was, "I wasn't raised like this. I am not supposed to be in here. My grandma didn't raise me like this. She raised me in church." She was very angry that her grandmother had lost the family home in a sale after LaVerne had gone to prison. She couldn't help her grandmother with her dementia and felt the loss of the family home was her fault. She was struggling to forgive others and was acting out which was pushing back her release date. I was overjoyed to see LaVerne several times at Bible studies. At the last one in June, she took the pulpit to share some news. She shared that her release date was up and that she had seen the address they were releasing her to. She went to correct the mistake, explaining that her grandmother's house had been sold from under her. The parole officer then explained that the address was for a halfway house LaVerne would be living at. Can you believe that the house was one and the same!

From the pulpit LaVerne praised God's holy name, explaining that her family home was exactly where she was heading and that God had taken care of her. She was, in fact, humbled by this and overjoyed at God's plan. The anger had lifted and she was able to see God's love and provision for her.

What else can I share about ministry in prison at a four-day intensive? The first introductions are very guarded. Women say hello but eye contact may be rare. Touch, other than a business handshake, is strictly forbidden. Not allowed. Women are placed at a table with two volunteers. My table had wonderful women, each with her own story and hopes, each with her own regrets and knowledge of God. Three at my table had very limited knowledge of God so this experience was perfect for them! We taught on several subjects including: "Making Choices," "The Prodigal Son," "Who is the Church?," "Discovery through Study," "Christian Action," and the two heavy hitters: "Forgiveness of Self" and "Forgiveness of Others." Alicia laughed the first three days then was so somber on the last day realizing this was real life we were dealing with! She has a three-year-old son and her husband and his parents are Christians and were really encouraging her to attend this program. She wants to get clean for her son! Joanne surprised me. She had no formal religious background and had been an enabled heroin addict most of her life. This was her third time in prison and she shared that she would rather be incarcerated than possibly OD'd on the outside.

Coming home from the prison is surreal. Driving on the highway west towards the mountains knowing that the women haven't been in a car for years or decades really hits me. I have been further in the past ten minutes than most of then have been in ten years. Seeing my kids and husband that night reminds me of what we take for granted. The women always comment on the fresh veggies and fruit we bring since the prison provides only frozen or canned produce. Even the cuddles of my dog feel new.

THE CHURCH INSIDE

The church inside is not so different from the church outside. Both consist of earnest and eager committed members, teachers' pets that raise their hands for every volunteer opportunity, visitors that find themselves needing entertainment so think they would check things out, socialites that want to look good more than be good, and those that want to eat the good food. The following saying about church makes me say "Hmmm . . .?" out loud. We are called to offer church from the nursery to the nursing home. OK, yes. And in the meantime we will also offer it behind locked doors as well. As the church we must adapt.

I have also been asked what leads to prison and what helps a person once they are released. Community. Most people find themselves making very poor choices because of their close relationships with other very emotionally unhealthy people. Unable to find the courage to leave the situation, or in actual fear of their lives, women often succumb to the life of crime while in these relationships. A second reason crime might occur is when a woman makes a small mistake and gets her kids taken away from her care. Without the children in her presence as a comfort and reason to make healthy choices, many experience great distress and make the worst choices imaginable, leading to years and decades away from their children.

Our hope is to speak truth, to reframe the truth so that the person imprisoned can see freedom even within the confines of bars and concrete walls. Stumbling blocks become stepping stones to a life worth living. Impact. Engage.

3

The Mission Field of Hospital Chaplaincy

MELINA DEZHBOD

INTRODUCTION

LIVING IN THE IN-BETWEEN space of life and death, and getting to walk alongside people in the journey, is truly a calling. As a chaplain, sometimes it's hard to put into words, but if I had to metaphorically explain the experience, to my Christian brain, it often feels like being in a perpetual cycle of Lent, Good Friday, and Easter. This very linear space of waiting, suffering, and the light at the end of the tunnel in a constant loop like a broken record is the daily reality I enter, sometimes within just an hour. However, unlike a broken record, each encounter is different, with no guarantees of what lies ahead. This is the routine of a hospital chaplain. Contrary to the portrayal in an episode of *Grey's Anatomy*, which some days does feel very real while working in the hospital, I hope that by bearing with me, you will gain a glimpse into the mission field of hospital chaplaincy by the end of this essay.

There is an adrenaline that hits after a full trauma is called. As you absorb the description of what to expect while rushing to the emergency room, anticipation collides with adrenaline. "What awaits me? God grant me the strength to navigate this situation," I silently pray. ETA: ten minutes. As the responding chaplain, I shuffle through the crowd of professionals (doctors, nurses, respiratory therapists, and X-ray techs) finding my spot outside the trauma room. The surge of adrenaline and anticipation momentarily halts as we await what's about to emerge through the ambulance bay. A moment of calm before the storm radiates through the hallways. In that moment, I assess who is present, observing the reactions of their unspoken body language. I then work to make myself known and available, addressing any patients who happen to be around and wondering what is unfolding. As patients and staff look at my badge and nod, I am assured of the importance of my presence in that moment. While I am uncertain of how I'll serve as a chaplain during the trauma, whether offering solace after a loss or supporting a family facing life-altering news, I am aware of the crucial role I play as part of the interdisciplinary team.

Though chaplains play a crucial part in healthcare, sometimes what we do may be misunderstood. People can associate the chaplain as the angel of death or the grim reaper. Walking into a room and stating, "I am the chaplain," more times than not, faces become flush, and people wonder, "Why am I seeing the chaplain?" Another common assumption is that our sole duty is to move around and pray for individuals. While both scenarios do reflect certain aspects of the role of a hospital chaplain, these tasks only scratch the surface of what it truly entails. Although carrying a staff and rocking a majestic black cape or spending the day in constant prayer may seem like a cool job, it doesn't quite capture the essence of journeying with people through the cycle of Lent, Good Friday, and Easter that I am referring to. The mission field of hospital chaplaincy goes much deeper than death and prayer alone. It encompasses the sorrow, the change, the recovery, the healing, the beauty, the ugliness, and the injustices, crafting a holy and sacred space. So, if we are more than just the grim reaper or the prayer warrior, and our work fosters the sacred and holy, then what exactly are we? What defines a hospital chaplain?

WHAT IS A HOSPITAL CHAPLAIN?

In my second year of seminary, the task of finding a clinical pastoral education (CPE) site became the focus of my year. I was one of the few classmates who decided to fulfill this canonical requirement for the ordination process in my second year versus my first. At the time, COVID was at its height, and I was unsure if I would land a CPE site. Some people found online programs, and with relief, I finally landed an internship at Yale New Haven Hospital in Connecticut. Only a few weeks before the program began, I found out that due to COVID, the program would not continue as planned.

Instead, I was transferred to the program at Bridgeport Hospital, which is a level 2 trauma center with the only burn unit in Connecticut. I had no idea what to expect, but I remember being told by classmates that it would be a life-altering experience. After forty-plus hours a week, multiple on-calls, lots of educational opportunities from didactics/supervision/IPR, learning to be a chaplain for staff and patients during COVID, and seeing a variety of cases, I thought I understood what it meant to be a hospital chaplain. To be honest, that intense summer, as I look back now, I realize I only got a small preview of what it truly means. It took my first unit, then a whole year of residency at Danbury Hospital in Connecticut, to working as a professional chaplain at a level 1 trauma center in Hartford, Connecticut, where I could confidently define the work of hospital chaplains.

The reality of chaplaincy, especially hospital chaplaincy, is that it's not always well defined. This lack of clarity poses a significant obstacle that continues to impact the work we do. People often receive incomplete or fragmented information due to variations in practices across different institutions, leading to potential misinterpretations or lost nuances in translation. Recognizing this challenge has encouraged a rise in dedicated research on chaplaincy. The hope is that increased research efforts and greater coherence in defining the role of chaplains will lead to better utilization of our services and recognition as professionals, like doctors, social workers, and nurses. Additionally, this would eliminate any doubts about why a chaplain is present during a medical emergency or why resources should be allocated to our departments. While the complexity of this topic merits its own chapter, I believe it is important to touch upon it here. As I share insights about the mission field of hospital chaplaincy, it's crucial to address the ongoing developments in this field. With that said, I want to take some time to explain what a hospital chaplain is and why you or your loved ones might encounter one during a hospital stay.

A hospital chaplain is an individual who holds a master's or PhD in divinity, theology, spirituality, religion, or a related field. They typically complete an internship unit of clinical pastoral education (CPE) and a year of residency. Most are in the process of becoming board certified, which is the licensing process for chaplains. A hospital chaplain undergoes extensive training and education to practice safely with people. In "Defining and Operationalizing Chaplain Presence: A Review," Adams reminds us that the Association of Professional Chaplains (APC) defines chaplaincy as follows:

> The ministry of chaplains includes a wide repertoire of services, including pastoral presence, pastoral conversations, pastoral/spiritual care, and pastoral counseling. Experiencing such services, patients, families, healthcare staff, and employees feel affirmed, understood, and supported in their particular predicament and in their right to have a particular ethical perspective. Those involved in the process can be enabled to explore the relationship of the physical issues of health and illness, psychological dimensions of the situation, i.e., anxiety, fear, trust, etc., and the spiritual issues i.e., meaning, hope, ultimate concern, and God's presence. Issues vary greatly from person to person depending upon the situation and belief system of the individual. Pastoral/spiritual care offers support for all involved and creates an atmosphere of sensitivity and trust in the context of healthcare ethics decision-making.[1]

This general definition explains the multifaceted ways chaplains engage with individuals and larger systems, cultivating opportunities to explore, question, and identify areas of distress, change, and need. Whether it's an unexpected or extended hospital stay or working through an intense twelve-hour shift, these situations often touch upon ethical and existential concerns, intertwining themes of spirituality, morals, and emotional well-being, among others.

Furthermore, this description develops into the foundational role of chaplains in a hospital setting. It is practiced and expanded upon as hospital chaplains serve on the multidisciplinary team, providing care to the overall hospital system. Chaplains may specialize in particular areas such as psychology, oncology, palliative care, hospice, or pediatrics. In hospitals, they possess a comprehensive understanding, enabling them to offer professional support across various domains, particularly when on call and covering the entire hospital. The day-to-day services they provide may include 24/7 coverage, spiritual and emotional support through assessment, response to codes/crises, sacramental requests, grief/loss/end-of-life care, participation in hospital committees, and involvement in organ donation/ethical cases.[2] The outcomes of their presence, guidance, and support enable people to identify supports, spiritual practices, coping resources, healthy/unhealthy behaviors, and storytelling, creating space for meaning-making, perspective, and relief in situations that could be overwhelming or

1. Adams, "Defining," 1247.
2. White et al., "Provision."

life-changing for patients, families, and even healthcare providers.[3] Recent research is continuing to show that chaplains are positively impacting the overall quality of care.

Hopefully, it is becoming more evident that chaplains are an essential part of healthcare. Hospital chaplains often operate as a sounding board, providing reason and harmony amidst the disruption and devastation. I have heard many patients describe a chaplain as a part of the family, especially when receiving the worst news of their lives. I have also heard staff express how the presence of the chaplain during a crisis has provided comfort and reassurance. Defining what we do and who we are is just the initial step in understanding the mission field of hospital chaplaincy. The next piece of the puzzle involves illustrating how beautifully this role plays out in service to those we care for.

THE DIVERSITY IN WHAT WE SEE AND WHO WE SERVE

Most professions adhere to a set of standards and ethics, and chaplaincy is no exception. When working with people at vulnerable stages of life, it becomes vital to avoid causing harm. Our training prepares us to self-supervise, holding ourselves accountable and aware of factors such as transference, bias, and proselytization, among others, in order to better serve patients, families, and staff. As stated in the preamble of the Common Code of Ethics for Chaplains, "Pastoral Counselors, Pastoral Educators, and Students, as spiritual care professionals, we affirm the dignity and value of each individual, respect the right of each faith group to hold its values and traditions, advocate for professional accountability that protects the public and advances the profession, and respect the cultural, ethnic, gender, racial, sexual orientation, and religious diversity of other professionals and those served, striving to eliminate discrimination."[4] It is only when we uphold and fully live by the values of our ethical standards that we can truly embody the characteristics of a chaplain. This includes and is not limited to: "Sen sitivity to the level of interaction needed; being positive and hopeful but with regard to patient suffering at the given moment; a consistently calm, gentle, and respectful demeanor; ability to listen and follow the patient's lead without being too talkative or assertive; and demonstrate compassion

3. Cunningham et al., "Perceptions."

4. Constituent Boards of the Council on Collaboration, "Common," 2.

and empathy without judgment."[5] As a hospital chaplain, I cannot undertake my daily functions without continuous self-work, adherence to the code of ethics, and striving to be a safe space where people can express themselves and their situations.

Entering a room as a hospital chaplain always entails caution, recognizing that it is not our space but rather a space into which we are invited. We seek permission to enter, sit down, and proceed with the visit, serving anyone and everyone who wishes to have us be a part of their journey. As an Episcopal priest in the hospital, I no longer present myself exclusively as the person with the collar or the theologian about to teach a forum. Instead, my Christian values are the groundwork from which I operate, becoming a vessel and instrument of love, healing, and hope—in turn, providing whatever the person in the room requires in that moment of encounter. One day, I may serve as the chaplain for a Catholic patient seeking a referral to see a Catholic priest; the next day for a spiritual but not religious individual in need of meditation; and another day, for someone grappling with existential questions as they face death. The beauty of being a hospital chaplain lies in engaging with people from all walks of life, where each day and each visit is unique. Diversity permeates every aspect of the work that hospital chaplains do, and it is our responsibility to ensure that this diversity is respected, protected, and nurtured. While I cannot claim to be a perfect chaplain and acknowledge that I make mistakes, reverencing human dignity remains fundamental in how I function in this position.

Research supports the idea that chaplains should be available for everyone, whether connecting individuals with a particular resource or providing a presence that allows people to explore their feelings about their existing circumstances. Research also indicates that including chaplains as full members of care teams, even for those who do not express religious or spiritual views, has been found to be valuable.[6] The observable and consistent characteristics of chaplains and their interaction style contribute to their effectiveness, supported by both quantitative and qualitative data.[7] Our training, code of ethics, and responsibilities empower us to meet people where they are, accompanying them based on their requests and preferences.

5. Adams, "Defining," 1250.

6. Cunningham et al., "Perceptions," 1244.

7. Cunningham et al., "Perceptions," 1244.

The portrayal of a hospital chaplain can be compared to that of a chameleon, able to adapt and become a part of different environments. Similarly, chaplains can enter various spaces, assess the situation, adapt, and assist. They do this in a way that is tailored to the individual they are with, thereby coming alongside them. This demonstrates one of the ways in which I perceive the mission field of chaplaincy in hospitals. Hospital chaplains can connect with individuals while maintaining a degree of distance from everyday systems. They are trained to lead and guide conversations, yet they are not therapists, religious leaders from home, or family members. However, they can temporarily and safely assume these roles as needed, offering support in moments, such as when one receives a stage four cancer diagnosis, or grapples with the decision of whether to remove their family from life support, or when their specific holiday must be spent in the emergency room away from loved ones. It's extended in times of heart-wrenching loss, like the death of a newborn baby, and in the aftermath of losing your first patient in a code blue. These examples represent just a fraction of the individuals and situations that a chaplain serves and engages with in the hospital setting.

HOW IS A HOSPITAL A MISSION FIELD FOR CHAPLAINCY?

My understanding of a mission field has been molded through a Christian lens, formed and reformed by both personal and professional experiences. From a very young age, I was taught that the essence of being a Christian is to exemplify and spread love to the best of one's ability wherever one finds oneself. Love was the mission, and the field was wherever you stood. I witnessed this principle in action when Episcopalians reached out across the globe to support my family's journey to the US. Instead of being preached at, we were given the space to find safety and practice our beliefs.

So, while my mind automatically turns to Mark 16:15 (NRSV), "Go into all the world and preach the gospel to all creation," when considering the mission field, my heart finds solace in John 14:27 (NRSV): "Peace I leave with you; my peace I give you. I do not give to you as the world gives. Do not let your hearts be troubled and do not be afraid." The innate message lies in this peace that surpasses all understanding. I used to believe it only pertained to finding meaning, purpose, and having life mostly figured out, which it does. However, since life is always unpredictable, it also entails attaining a level of peace where, no matter life's challenges, a sense of stillness can carry you through.

Undeniably, the hospital is a mission field, giving opportunities to live out one's faith and values, bringing hope in seemingly hopeless situations, spreading love in the hardest moments, and offering comfort amidst fear and uncertainty. It's about living out the gospel not just through words but through actions. Additionally, it shows how the pursuit of peace is ongoing. In most of my interactions, whether it's a routine procedure like a knee replacement or a devastating loss after a loved one fails to return from a CAT scan, people are grappling with how to navigate life, seeking peace and finding guidance in their beliefs. In essence, this is where the role of a chaplain becomes vital, and the mission field of hospital chaplaincy holds parallels to the cycle of Lent, Easter, and Good Friday. As the hospital chaplain you will support and walk with people through the waiting, death, and some form of good news.

Similar to going through a Holy Week, people need reminders of something larger than themselves, especially in times of turmoil and despair. They need messengers to accompany them through their journey of questioning, searching, and feeling overwhelmed by emotions. This continues to be the present and future of spiritual leadership—an age-old concept that often goes unnoticed. It's easy and normal to become consumed by religious routines, forgetting that the greatest need and work lie in places like the hospitals in our communities. We don't always have to travel far to be part of something greater or to fulfill the call of spreading and bringing good news. Sometimes, it's right outside or even inside the doors of our churches, synagogues, or temples.

In the hospital, dignity for all is the mission, the hospital itself is the field, and chaplains are the trained spiritual professionals, representing various backgrounds, including atheists, who make this mission possible. They serve as bridges connecting patients, families, and staff to their social and belief systems, creating spaces where hope, reconciliation, healing, and peace can be experienced or sought after. This deep connection fosters something sacred and divine. Whether one names it God, nature, kindness, or the universe, the divine presence is profound and present in hospitals, and while I may be just one voice, I witness it regularly. As stated in "Provision of Chaplaincy Services in U.S. Hospitals: A Strategic Conformity Perspective," "Patients who receive spiritual care report better hospital experience, improvements in mental and spiritual wellbeing, decrease in anxiety, and improve quality of life."[8] The hospital chaplain paves the way for the life-and-death work being carried out in hospitals by grounding their institutions in their mission, being accountable for the numerous disparities in healthcare, and remembering why each of us was called to our field of work.

GUIDANCE OF THE SPIRIT

I vividly recall my first on-call experience as a chaplain intern during a day shift. A page from the NICU made my heart drop. Upon arrival, I found myself faced with the urgent need to perform an emergency baptism. Fortunately, an incredible nurse provided step-by-step guidance, easing my uncertainty. When I completed the baptism, she asked how I knew what to say and pray. Truthfully, I didn't know myself. Most chaplains will attest that often, words fail in such moments, and what unfolds is guided by the work of the Spirit. I do not navigate these situations alone; it is through the Spirit that this work becomes possible for me.

I have witnessed the right chaplain on call during crises that needed them and their gifts. I have seen families praying in tongues, holding on to hope, laying their hand on a patient's foot as they are resuscitated, only to be brought back miraculously after forty minutes. I have observed elders supporting a grieving family after the sudden loss of a toddler. Nurses, regardless of their faith, have sought out chaplains to cleanse a room after the passing of a patient. These experiences reveal something greater at play. While I cannot explain why certain events occur while others do not, and some remain as tragic as ever with no silver lining, I firmly believe that the hospital environment is not a mere coincidence. There is an intangible energy, both positive and negative, coursing through its rooms and hallways, often unspoken but profound. Consequently, this is why I cannot go through a day without the guidance of the Holy Spirit, and why prioritizing self-care becomes imperative.

SELF-CARE IN THIS LINE OF WORK

As a chaplain, I am trained to be an interfaith spiritual leader. I do not enter a room ready to pray in the name of Jesus, nor do I carry a Bible with

8. White, "Provision," 342.

the intention to share verses with everyone I meet. Instead, I offer support personalized to individuals from diverse faith backgrounds, traditions, or those with no faith. Our role is to facilitate personal exploration of faith and belief through appropriate assessment and to refer to hospital and community resources when necessary.

Subsequently, this portion of the essay reflects only my perspective on navigating this mission field and cannot be generalized for every hospital chaplain. While my primary duty is to provide support, my effectiveness is deeply rooted in my own tradition. Balancing this with the demands of chaplaincy took time but became a priority for me. The extensiveness of experiences in a single day is immense, often moving from one form of suffering to another. It is easy to become overwhelmed and burned-out, challenges inherent in healthcare. This emphasizes the importance of spiritual, physical, and emotional self-care.

Personally, I have established a prayer routine upon arriving and leaving work, seeking comfort in the chapel on difficult days. As I drive home, I leave a window open to symbolically release the day's weight. Being a constant source of support necessitates replenishing my own mind, body, and spirit.

A DAY IN THE LIFE OF A HOSPITAL CHAPLAIN

The best way for me to portray what I am speaking about is by sharing a day in my life. I will use a day that had many extremes, noting that it's not always like this. Some days are calm, some days I am mostly declined, and then there are the unforgettable days. In order to remain compliant with HIPAA and privacy protocols, details of certain cases have been altered.

I was working the night shift. I got ready and left my house by 5:50 p.m. During my drive, I recited my routine prayers for the shift, the people I may encounter, and whatever else was on my mind. Thankfully, it was a work night, so I could park on campus; otherwise, I would have had to add half an hour to my commute just to be shuttled to the hospital. I arrived by 6:50 p.m., and the evening chaplain gave me the report and passed the pager. At 7 p.m., the first call came in, a code blue. I made my way up and provided a supportive presence. I checked in with the nurse who shared that the family was present. I walked to the family room and sat with them, offering hospital updates and prayers. As I went back and forth, bringing any news or updates, the family anxiously awaited. When the doctor delivered the news that the patient had passed, I found myself holding the spouse as they collapsed in tears on the floor. I stayed with that family for two hours. Somewhere in between, a trauma case came in. I made a phone call to the ED to inform them that I was with a grieving family and to only page me for emergencies. Being the only chaplain, I found myself triaging what needed my immediate care and attention. Once the family was more settled, I walked back down to my office. I checked my list of consults and followed up on the trauma, which was a motor vehicle accident with no immediate needs. By now, it was almost 10 p.m., and I had charted my previous visits. Then, a rapid response was called around 10:30 p.m. I headed up to the floor where the family was present. As the patient was being assessed, I introduced myself to the family. Since this family was the primary health representative, they were providing medical information to the doctors. After introducing myself, I remained quiet until the doctors left. Once the other medical staff had cleared the room, I listened to the patient's life story and explored the fears of each family member after witnessing their loved one's sudden allergic reaction. After providing emotional support, they settled, and I walked back to the office.

As I walked back, I received a page around 12:15 a.m. to provide support to a patient in the ICU. When I arrived, I found the patient anxious and unsure of my presence because they were not religious. As I explained my role, the patient became more comfortable and shared about their accident that had changed their life. They were able to find comfort in meditation and were open to doing one together. After the meditation, the patient settled, and I walked back to the office. As I noticed a calm in now what was the day, I made my way down to the ED and began visiting with whoever was awake. I provided water, blankets, and crackers for those unable to sleep or waiting for tests or to be moved in-patient. It was around 1:50 a.m. when I heard a bunch of loud noises. The intercom went off, requesting immediate staff support. Every staff member started running in the direction of the call, and someone was rushed into the trauma room, leaving a trail of blood as they were rushed back from triage. As all hands were on deck, the emergency room went into lockdown. I made my way around, providing support to everyone who witnessed this and was either scared or in shock. During this chaos, a full trauma was called, pagers were going off, and more staff were arriving in the trauma bay. With no family present, both patients were immediately taken to surgery for gunshot injuries. It was now 3:30 a.m., the emergency room had calmed down again, and most people were sleeping. I finished my rounds, and I decided to use my break to close my eyes for a little while.

As I rested my eyes, a page came in from the ICU around 4:45 a.m. The family of one of the gunshot victims had arrived, and I went up to provide support. The family was unsure if the patient would make it and needed to discuss the next steps regarding goals of care. They didn't identify with any faith or religion but talking it out was what they needed in the moment. It was now about 6 a.m.; I got my paperwork and notes ready for the day chaplain to hand over the pager at 7 a.m. I was able to use the rest of the morning to respond to emails. At that point, I was tired and very much done with the shift. I was thankful no more calls came in. After handing the pager over, I couldn't even make it to the chapel. My words wouldn't come out, and all I wanted to do was get to my car, do my forty-five-minute drive home, and sleep. I drove home with my windows open and in silence, and my prayer was, "Jesus, you know what is on my heart; please take the day." This is a day in the life of a chaplain at a level 1 trauma center.

HEAR IT FROM A HOSPITAL CHAPLAIN

As a hospital chaplain working in challenging mission fields, I am deeply grateful for the support that surrounds me. Without the guidance and inspiration of mentors, colleagues, and my own family, I would not be the chaplain I am today. My journey has been shaped by the wisdom of seasoned chaplains who have nurtured and educated me. Currently, I am part of an incredible spiritual care department where colleagues support each other and excel in their expertise. My father, a priest and hospice chaplain with two decades of experience, has been a profound influence on my vocation. As I began writing, I knew that their voices must be heard.

I asked each of them, "What does it mean to be a hospital chaplain?"

And they replied:

Rev. Winston Wilks:

> It means to provide pastoral and spiritual support to patients and staff when they are experiencing unexpected life changes. A hospital chaplain also provides compassion in the midst of others' chaos, while providing empathic listening, affirmation of patients'

value, perspective, and experiences, and exploration of sources of their strength.

Rev. Carol Pusey, MDiv, BCC Staff Chaplain:

Being a hospital chaplain means to me that I get the opportunity to be invited into the sacred spaces of others. To be that calm, compassionate, listening presence for them as they express their concerns and feelings, and to hold space in those crucial moments as they process those feelings.

Zento Ryan Weeks (Zen Buddhist):

For me, being a hospital chaplain means showing up for people and believing whatever their story is. Then showing them deep compassion by going alongside them. And working with the hospital staff to coordinate care for them or advocate for them, while providing our presence and example to the staff. We are not just priests anymore; we are professional people that really care.

Bethany Astrachan Per Diem Multi-Faith Chaplain, St. Francis Hospital:

Chaplaincy has helped me to integrate many parts of myself. Personal wounds have healed. Life aspirations have been discovered and acted upon. In sum, my personal theology has found expression.

Very Reverend Marc A. Vranes, MDiv:

Mine is a bivocational priesthood. I am an ordained Orthodox priest, and work in Catholic healthcare as a chaplain. There is rarely a degree of separation between the two. I am not one without being the other, both at the same time. The blessings of being a hospital chaplain is that it allows me to minister to whoever God puts in my life. Chaplaincy has improved my listening skills as I am engaged in interfaith dialogue which allows for much personal spiritual growth. My role is not to convert, but to uplift others and encounter them wherever they are emotionally and spiritually at any given moment.

Rev. Esmail Dezhbod:

> As a hospice chaplain who meets people in their homes, facilities, and hospitals, one of the most valuable skills we possess is the ability to offer a silent presence, engage in empathic listening, and validate the grief they are experiencing. Dying is a holy time, and it is an honor to accompany patients and families as their loved ones transition to a different stage of life.

Denise Wolferman:

> Being a hospital chaplain is a sacred honor that is a window into the Divine. We are witness to miracles every day. From the people that walk away from horrific accidents to courageous families that give the gift of life to strangers out of the ashes of devastating tragedies to a loving family gathered to say goodbye at the end of a well-lived life, we are given a window into G-d's holiness in everyday life, and it is a privilege.

Without the dedicated service of chaplains who make significant sacrifices to professionally serve, the mission field of hospital chaplaincy would be nonexistent.

CONCLUSION: THE REVELATION OF HOSPITAL CHAPLAINCY

The true mission field of the hospital and chaplaincy is this: Wherever you are called, you go, and whoever needs your services, you serve. There are limits, but in spiritual care departments, they are not bound by walls, agendas, or exclusion. Chaplaincy is evolving and reaching people in high numbers daily. A reformation of the future of faith is being formed through chaplaincy. Specifically, hospital chaplains are establishing frameworks for spiritual and religious support, catering to individuals who maintain, have never attended, or have ceased attending religious institutions.

We have much to learn from chaplains, who serve as the past, present, and future pioneers of ensuring widespread access to spiritual, emotional, and moral support across various sectors including healthcare, education, sports, the military, government, and beyond. The mission field of hospitals and chaplaincy captures only a glimpse of the various ways chaplains tend to their communities and impact numerous situations and lives. Nonetheless, the hospital chaplain paves a way, extending support to the multitude. In other words, I can confidently define a chaplain working in the mission field of a hospital as someone who, with the guidance of the divine, their colleagues, and their training, can take seven loaves of bread and one fish, and provide nourishment for most of those they encounter.

Having chaplains in the mission field of hospitals is both a gift and a necessity. Hospital chaplains possess the ability to discern where love remains, break down barriers that hinder hope, and offer grace in what can feel like seemingly impossible situations. Like other healthcare professionals, they are continuously learning, growing, and advocating for the future of their field, striving to provide the best care possible. Therefore, let us not forget about the hospital chaplain who navigates the demanding yet rewarding mission field of a hospital daily.

BIBLIOGRAPHY

Adams, Kevin. "Defining and Operationalizing Chaplain Presence: A Review." *Journal of Religion and Health* 58 (2019) 1246–58.

Constituent Boards of the Council on Collaboration. "Common Code of Ethics for Chaplains, Pastoral Counselors, Pastoral Educators and Students." Apchaplains.org. https://www.apchaplains.org/wp-content/uploads/2022/05/Common-Code-of-Ethics.pdf.

Cunningham, Christopher J. L., et al. "Perceptions of Chaplains' Value and Impact Within Hospital Care Teams." *Journal of Religion Health* 56 (2017) 1231–47.

White, Kelsey B., et al. "Provision of Chaplaincy Services in U.S. Hospitals: A Strategic Conformity Perspective." *Health Care Manage Rev.* 48 (2023) 342–52.

4

Islamic Perspective on Elderly Care

SYAZANA DURRANI

INTRODUCTION

> Sajda Khan and her husband Rahmat opened Fonthill Gardens, a six-bed assisted living home in Hawthorne, California, for the Los Angeles area's aging Muslim population. They found a contractor to provide halal meats, included a prayer room, and made enthusiastic presentations to area mosques. A year later they have cared for two Christians and one Buddhist, but no Muslims.
>
> "People feel that others will criticize them," said Mrs. Khan, who is from Pakistan. "You know, 'So and so left her mother in a facility, and now look at her looking fashionable at the mall.' It's very frustrating."

The snippet above illustrates the reality of the Islamic perspective of elderly care. Muslims see institutional placement for elders as a form of neglect and abandonment.[1] The reason for this has its roots in the guiding principle of Muslims which is the Quran and Sunnah.[2] No matter the flavor and cultural expression of Islam a practicing Muslim observes, the fundamental understanding of the faith regarding the elderly is best captured in the expression of "birr ul-walidayn," meaning being dutiful to parents. Religiously, Islam places supreme importance on the rights of parents and their care, second only to the obligation of Tauheed, or "Oneness of God,"

1. Clemetson, "Homes."
2. Al-Heeti, "Nursing," 209.

as evident in numerous Quranic verses: "Be grateful to Me and to both your parents";[3] "Your Lord has decreed that you worship none but Him and be kind to your parents";[4] "Worship God and ascribe not partners unto Him. And be virtuous toward parents and kinsfolk."[5]

Prioritizing the treatment of parents, second only to obeying God, translates to Muslims placing such importance on filial duty. On one occasion, Muhammad was asked: "O Allah's Messenger, which of the deeds is best?" The Prophet replied: "Prayer at its correct time." He was asked: "Then what?" He replied: "Good treatment of parents." He was asked: "Then what?" He replied: "Striving in Allah's cause." On yet another occasion, it is reported that the Prophet asked his companions: "Shall I tell you what are the greatest of major sins? To attribute partners to God and to be disrespectful toward parents."[6]

The dignity and the rights of elders are such an integral part of Islamic belief and practice. The Quran emphasizes the opportunity to be good to parents in old age for the "weakness upon weakness" mothers bore in pregnancy, and the exhaustion of raising children.[7] Islamic scholarship consents that mothers deserve the best companionship, followed by the father, due to the birth and postnatal burdensome tasks mothers undertake: "A man came to the Prophet and said, 'O Messenger of God! Who among the people is the most worthy of my good companionship? The Prophet said: 'Your mother.' The man said, 'Then who?' The Prophet said: 'Then your mother.' The man further asked, 'Then who?' The Prophet said: 'Then your mother.' The man asked again, 'Then who?' The Prophet said: 'Then your father.'"[8]

Islam also sanctions tremendous patience in dealing with parents, whereby the Quran emphatically stresses: "If either or both of them reach old age with you, do not even say 'uff!' to them or scold them, but speak to them in terms of honor and kindness. Lower to them the wing of humility, and say, 'My Lord, Have mercy on them, for they did care for me when I was young.'"[9] The *Study Quran* commentary clarifies extensively the idea of "Uff!":

3. Nasr, *Study Quran* 31:14.
4. Nasr, *Study Quran* 17:23.
5. Nasr, *Study Quran* 4:36.
6. *Ṣaḥīḥ al-Bukhārī* 527.
7. *Ṣaḥīḥ al-Bukhārī* 5977.
8. *Ṣaḥīḥ al-Bukhārī* 5971; *Ṣaḥīḥ Muslim* 2548.
9. Nasr, *Study Quran* 17:24–25.

> Uff! can be an expression of complaint or annoyance, and the implication here is that one should be tolerant and patient with parents and their needs and dependencies, just as they were patient with one as a child. More specifically, uff can refer to something that is filthy or soiling, and some thus suggest that the verse is addressing the irritation a son or daughter might feel in having to assist elderly parents with personal hygiene. The prohibition against saying Uff! to one's parents may also be meant to discourage the use of any kind of ugly, harsh, or dismissive expression with them. To chide them may also mean to rebuff them or turn away from them in anger.[10]

The commentary above displays that the Islamic tradition highlights frailty as part of old age. Mental and physical decline is par for the course, where Quranic verses describe the final stage of life as one of weakness and regression.[11] Elders as wisdom holders corresponds to Quranic value in viewing earthly life stages as a means to be mindful of exiting the physical world through death and contemplating on the resurrection. Zechariah's reflections on his old age relay this: "My Lord! Truly, my bones have weakened, and my head glistens with white hair. Yet, my Lord, I have never been disappointed in my prayer to you. Truly, I fear my relatives after me, and my wife is barren. So grant me, from Your Presence, an heir."[12] Zechariah's fear of his relatives relates to his concern that there is no one worthy to guide the religious community or uphold the religion properly after his death, thus his supplication for a worthy inheritor. This ties in aptly with another oft-repeated hadith where the Prophet says: "When a man dies, his deeds come to an end except for three things: Sadaqah Jariyah (ceaseless charity); a knowledge which is beneficial, [*sic*] or a virtuous descendant who prays for him (for the deceased)."[13]

The status and presence of elders as a reminder of our mortality is a holy opportunity to receive blessings from God. The hadith that speaks to this is the Prophet's reminder that heaven is underneath mothers' feet.[14] Tying suffering to worship is a fundamental Islamic practice and perception. God's grace is sought not only through one's situation in the physical world, but

10. Nasr, *Study Quran* 701.
11. Nasr, *Study Quran* 36n68.
12. Nasr, *Study Quran* 19:4–5. Author's paraphrase.
13. *Riyad as-Salihin* 1383.
14. *Sunan al-Nasāʾī* 3104.

also for the hereafter. The Prophet reminds, "The father is the middle door of Paradise. So it is up to you whether you take advantage of it or not."[15]

I was in my mid-thirties when I first interned as a chaplain student at a life-plan community for older adults where I live in Northern Virginia. I did not know what to expect or what I was getting myself into, so I plunged into the experience. I may have appeared younger than my age, because I received constant amazement and delight from the senior residents when I shared I had children ages eight and four. When my children attended my first clinical pastoral education (CPE) graduation, I received my first of much life wisdom from the senior residents: that I will soon have a teenager in my daughter. Of course, I did not hear it as a forewarning, nor did I even understand what it meant then. Yet, the caution is a lifeline during the turbulent teenage years my husband and I are going through with our daughter more than half a decade later. Those words of wisdom steadied me through the hormonal storms and daily clashes, and reminded me that the teenage years transcend time, family systems, cultures, languages—even technology—and that this season, too, will pass. These older adults knew what was awaiting me in the twenty-first century, from their own life experiences through the early and mid-twentieth century.

ORGANIZATIONAL SPIRITUAL CARE AND EDUCATION CONTEXT

Goodwin Living is a faith-based, not-for-profit senior living organization with historical roots tied to the Episcopal Church. It owns and operates three life-plan communities: Goodwin House Alexandria, Goodwin House Bailey's Crossroads, and The View Alexandria, along with Goodwin Living at Home, Goodwin Rehabilitation, and Goodwin Hospice and Palliative Care. Goodwin Living offers independent apartment living, assisted living, memory support, nursing care, home care, rehab, and hospice and palliative care, serving over 2,200 older adults and 900 staff members. The mission statement of Goodwin Living is simple and profound: "To support, honor and uplift the lives of older adults and those who care for them." Spirituality is highly valued, as is pluralism and a diversity of religious and spiritual expressions. A previous CEO once said she thought of "faith-based" not as specifically Episcopalian, but as a hopeful orientation towards the future.

15. *Sunan Ibn Mājah* 3663.

Tending to and providing spiritual care for the older adults and their caregivers is the backbone of the Goodwin Living Clinical Pastoral Education (CPE) program. Founded in 1998, the Goodwin Living CPE was developed with the vision to train faith leaders and educate spiritual caregivers to enter and stay in authentic, skillful, caring relationships with older adults. Goodwin Living communities resemble congregation settings where longer-term relationships are possible. Students accompany senior living residents on the spiritual journey in the last decades of life and, at times, the last weeks and days of life.

Goodwin Living CPE also has robust clinical placements. There has been a rich history of partnership with local faith communities, local and regional hospitals, hospices, and senior living communities to place students in learning contexts outside of Goodwin Living communities. This unique milieu provides a wide range of opportunities for Goodwin Living CPE students to practice spiritual care and counseling, including public worship, crisis intervention, grief support, group leadership, and pastoral ministry.

Goodwin Living CPE thus is unique with the program's focus on the spiritual journey of aging and end of life. Hospice chaplains trained through the program graduate ready to be hired on to a hospice team and thrive in all aspects of the role. The aging process has tremendous spiritual possibilities for the sharing of love, wisdom, family connections, and joys of life. Aging also inevitably contains spiritual pitfalls of despair, grief, dependence, frailty, dementia, and loss of identity. Students get a chance to minister with people living on this profound spectrum of spiritualities.

Students also get a chance to minister with Goodwin Living team members who come from all over the world, and to grapple with the justice issues that arise in senior living and healthcare in general in the United States. In senior living, often the most vulnerable members of society (underprivileged, immigrants, women) care for newly vulnerable members of society (aging, professional-class residents). Vulnerability is built into aging, and no one is spared from the need of care. At our best, a ministry of mutuality is a part of caring for older adults. Older adults largely do not want to be served; they want to be known and to come to know others. CPE students have the rich opportunity to walk alongside people of many different religious traditions, and of no religion; with people who come from or have lived all over the world and others who have been in Virginia all their lives; with diplomats and dishwashers; with former CEOs and current certified nursing assistants, licensed by the Virginia Board of Nursing.

It is the program's optimism that students become comfortable practicing their spiritual care craft, particularly in future ministry, where religious demographics in the United States lean older. With students' practice and familiarity with dementia, frailty and other ailments of old age, they learn to connect from the heart in the face of cognitive and/or physical differences. In understanding hospice and palliative care, CPE students who continue on their spiritual leadership mantle can become more equipped to accompany individuals and families navigate life permeated with realities of aging and death.

MUSLIM CHAPLAIN IN ELDERLY CARE SETTING

Having interned at Goodwin Living CPE program for six units of CPE and continuing with my current chaplain educator training meant that I "was raised" in the elderly caregiving context as my spiritual care training. Plunging into the deep well of spiritual care alongside older adults has been a gift, not only of time, but of gentle learning. I needed it. I learned to listen while I was also being listened to. I learned to accompany while I was also being accompanied. The program's proponent of ministry of mutuality means that, in terms of spiritual care, the residents seek to be known, as they also seek to know those who are caring for them.

This mutual care fits my constitution as a Southeast Asian Muslim woman who sees spiritual care as a neighborly act. My Asian value that places elders in high regard means that I am ever ready to learn from, listen to, and support the elders and their caregivers where needed. My Islamic heart cherishes spiritual care as a starting point to enjoin good: "O you who believe! . . . Help one another toward piety and reverence";[16] "Let there be among you a community calling to the good, enjoining right, and forbidding wrong. It is they who shall prosper."[17] Still, I began my CPE journey wide-eyed, because there is so much I did not know, especially in being with older adults with Alzheimer's and other forms of dementia.

Our program teaches Naomi Feil's Validation, a method for communicating with individuals diagnosed with Alzheimer's disease and related

16. Nasr, *Study Quran* 5:2.

17. Nasr, *Study Quran* 3:104.

dementias.[18] Using Erik Erikson's theory of Developmental Life Stages and Life Tasks, Feil encapsulates that each life stage comes with its own unique tasks that, when overlooked, will resurface and persist during "the old-old" Resolution Stage of Life.[19] From her decades-old working with old-old people, Feil observes their share of psychological and social needs, mainly in needing to resolve incomplete life tasks or imprisoned emotions during this Resolution Stage in order to die peacefully. Feil writes:

> Older people who are disoriented often lose their motivation to conform to social norms. Their failure to resolve important developmental tasks earlier in life catches up with them in old age. They return to the past to resolve these tasks. These old-old people no longer have the tools to cope with the ever-increasing changes of aging. As a result, they choose to retreat. . . . Disorientation in very old person [*sic*] may represent the normal struggle of the old-old person with recent memory loss, seeking to restore the past and heal old wounds before death.[20]

The humanistic principle of the Validation Method is an important starting point for students and spiritual care practitioners to cultivate the basic sense of awe and wonder in the life of the care-seekers. In the Islamic tradition, one of the three shortest chapters of the Quran is *Al Asr* (The Declining Day) with three verses: By the declining day, truly mankind is in loss, save those who believe, perform righteous deeds, exhort one another to truth, and exhort one another to patience.[21] Translated also as "time" or "afternoon," *asr* can be understood as the reality of the human condition that is subject to the decaying essence of time. The verses call for the meditation of decline and loss (truly mankind is in loss) as the reality of aging: from ability to disability, strength to weakness, cognition to memory loss, youth to frailty. Yet, the impending doom of human loss and decline affects the collective, save those who believe, and those who enjoin one another to good deeds, counsel one another toward the truth, and encourage one another to bear life difficulties with patience. In these "afternoons" of life transitions, the Validation Method calls for an opportunity for those caring and journeying alongside the elders to contemplate on aging as "signs of

18. Feil and Klerk-Rubin, "Validation," 40.
19. Feil and Klerk-Rubin, "Validation," 25–29
20. Feil and Klerk-Rubin, "Validation," 34.
21. Nasr, *Study Quran* 103:1–3.

God"[22] while practicing the soul-purifying exercise of *sabr*, or patience and performance of righteous deeds. Additionally, in enjoining the Validation Method, the old-old are also made space to practice returning to the innate human state: remembrance and innate dependency.

When I came to CPE, I came with an open heart to learn in relationship from and with educators and peers. While interpersonal skills is the footing of spiritual care, theories are the spine of CPE action-reflection-new action learning. Theories imparted and practiced in CPE are designed to contextualize the inexplicable enigma of one's beliefs and theology as well as one's spiritual, psychological, emotional, and social needs. It takes time for theories to seep in, to become second nature to my spiritual care and educational practice. The way theories enter my practice is like the practice of *dhikr*, or remembrance, of devotionals recited in remembrance of God.

Take Feil's Validation for example—the method breaks down engagement of empathy with the old-old explicitly, where "a validating caregiver accepts the physical deterioration of old-old persons; enter that person's world; and becomes a nurturing, trusted authority."[23] Feil educates and affirms that validating caregivers do not judge old-old's behaviors as inappropriate but necessary for healing and closure in their life's culmination. Through Feil's fourteen techniques of Validation,[24] caregivers have a framework to emotionally experience and contextualize the old-old's lived experience in exercising empathy. While "empathy" may not be the formal terminology used in Islamic discourse, the practice of empathy is a fundamental Islamic summons to being:

> The Prophet says, "None of you will have faith till he wishes for his brother what he likes for himself."[25]
>
> The Prophet said, "You see the believers as regards their being merciful among themselves and showing love among themselves and being kind, resembling one body, so that, if any part of the body is not well then the whole body shares the sleeplessness (insomnia) and fever with it."[26]

22. Nasr, *Study Quran* 41:53.
23. Feil and Klerk-Rubin, "Validation," 47.
24. Feil and Klerk-Rubin, "Validation," 49–50.
25. *Ṣaḥīḥ al-Bukhārī* 13.
26. *Ṣaḥīḥ al-Bukhārī* 6011.

Your creation and your uprising are as but one soul.[27]

I have come to see theories as practice and opportunity for self-knowledge: Whoever knows the mysteries of the spirit, knows himself. If he knows himself, he knows his Lord. The beauty of Islamic scholarship is her openness to wisdom wherever it originates. Feil's Validation Method and other theories practiced in our CPE program have been an unveiling of the human condition, including my own tendencies and functioning in interpersonal relationships. When veils are lifted, illusions fall away, and the inevitability of seeing things as they are is made manifest. What is left, thus, is my own self, carrying on with self-grace and compassion that I move in the world justly, wisely, beautifully. God willing.

CARING FOR THE CAREGIVERS OF THE ELDERLY

Goodwin Living's mission extends to support, honor, and uplift a global family of team members who represent more than sixty-five countries. This encompasses not only the healthcare staff, but also dining, environmental services, laundry, and facilities attendants, whom the pandemic has uncovered and redefined as essential workers. Department of Labor describes essential workers as the foundation to the nation's economy, and are "disproportionately low-paid workers, disproportionately women and workers of color."[28] This is also the reality at Goodwin Living residential communities. The direct care workforce at Goodwin Living represents the national phenomenon: comprised mainly of women immigrants with "higher percentages of higher education degrees and are generally older, with a median age of 48."[29] While I have been gifted to have my spiritual care training with older adults, the camaraderie of the immigrant health caregivers and essential workers has been my training sustenance. Many of the workers, including me, recognize that we are far away from home and are unable to be direct carers for our own family members in our home countries. And taking care of the elderly at the life-plan community soothes that responsibility and yearning pain, that the caregiving of our profession may have a karmic effect on our elderly loved ones in our birth countries. Many of the direct care workers immigrated from war-torn countries, with memories

27. Nasr, *Study Quran* 31:28.

28. US Department of Labor, "Essential."

29. Espinoza, "Immigrants."

and stories that endow them with natural gifts of empathy toward the old-old they care for. And those like me, who immigrate for opportunities and destinies, are deeply grounded in the intrinsic human value of our profession.

Providing spiritual care to our team members is the most beloved part of my job. These essential care providers are faithful people of all traditions, ethnic groups, family backgrounds, and identities. They want to share about their lives, their families, their work, their highlights and low points, their challenges and hearts' delights. Like the next person, they want to be seen in their authentic selves, and my spiritual care practice is only to affirm and invite such genuineness in the midst of our work and caregiving. With the team members I practice caring and being cared for as my whole self. And in return, I too am seen and known by these warm individuals. When I greet them, I greet their families and inquire about their health. We ask each other about our families locally and those in our birth countries. This exchange serves the important function of being seen as a sum of whom and where we come from. Being wholly ourselves is the starting point of the quality work I believe my coworkers and I provide in caring for our older adults.

WISDOM GLEANED FROM THE OLD

Take the most from life that you can, / Before you descend into the Dust below; / Sans wine, sans songs, / As Dust into Dust, under Dust you lie

—Omar Khayyam's *Rubai*[30]

Just like any other chaplaincy context with its intricacies, ministry with older adults comes with its own frequency and modulation. I share here some of the wisdom gleaned from my years training in spiritual care and sharing lives with older adults.

Slowing It Down

When I started my CPE journey, one of the first invitations given by my chaplain educator was to "slow it down." Never knowing what it meant truly other than trusting in the practice that I will reap its benefit eventually,

30. Fitzgerald, "Rubáiyát," 126.

I took careful stock of myself to slow. it. down. It is a practice at work to walk slowly, as our workspace is also a shared home space for the older adults living in the community. I have grown much from this gem of invitation. Walking intentionally and purposefully has a profoundly meditative effect. In slowing down my breath, my presence, I have become more well-practiced in being aware of my emotions and their impact. The practice of slowing it down also has shifted my perspective of quality caregiving from a quantified one. It brings up a reminder of the prophetic tradition: "If anyone of you leads the people in the prayer, he should shorten it for amongst them are the weak, the sick and the old."[31]

Hair While Aging

"My white hair is like frosting," says Mrs. E. Her words were a delight and helped me visualize aging heads like cupcakes with arrays of delectable, multicolored icing toppings. "What deliciousness!" I exclaimed. Mrs. E laughed, enjoying our shared imagination. From the elders, I am learning about my own aging progress. From the elders who welcome their aging transitions, I am modeled to strive to accept mine. From the elders who accept these transitions less so, they help normalize my resistance to change. Both intents have wisdom in the spectrum of human experience.

Forgetting, Precarious Memory

Maturing with aging elders, I become acquainted with the cosmos of forgetting and precarious memory. From these wisdom sages, I learn all the various strategies one engages in remembering. Ms. K's approach is having several different paper calendars in strategic places in the house to write down appointments and lunch dates. Mr. J relies on his iPad notifications to direct his day, week, month. Ms. N gratefully has a friend outside the community who calls to remind her of her schedules. As one whose heart inclines on *dhikr*, I find myself seeing and hearing these remembering tactics as part the domain of *dhikrs*. The Islamic practice of remembering is always and forevermore to bring us back to who we are, and who we are is where beauty and mercy resides.

31. *Ṣaḥīḥ al-Bukhārī* 671.

Time: "God's Waiting room," "The Green Mile"

Journeying with older adults brings to the forefront the famous saying that Sufis are children of time.[32] The recognition that "no one gets out of (this place) alive" can be both comforting and terrifying, as the elders make their final home transition to the senior living community. Many take it in stride and cope with some morbid humor—a resident wrote a play of this final-abode awareness titled *God's Waiting room* that has seen several performances by the play-reading group. For others, connecting movie pop culture to their living space gives credence to the choice of their final home. There is a part of the building with its green carpet and green wall on one side and outside greenery through the window wall on the other that warrants its nickname, "The Green Mile." The moniker comes from a similarly titled crime drama film on a prison's death row. This long "green" hallway connects the independent living building to the dining and other activity spaces. Hearing residents see the hallway as a death row march is a place where I see the elders doing the work of being present to death that is a surety for us all. The elders, who are sons and daughters of time, teach me how they befriend death in the daily.

> You should hold to the religion of old women. Learn from an old woman.[33]

Holding dear to the above wisdom, practicing spiritual care with older adults simply means that I listen intently to the life treasures generously shared and imparted. I was taught the Hail Mary invocation from Mrs. M, who has since passed. May Mother Mary love us and keep us. Celebrating Mr. K's ninety-ninth birthday with a cupcake and silence imparted deep presence I was fortunate to experience. Ms. C, Ms. B, and Ms. N tell me the minutiae of being a mother, and I receive their continued blessing and validation that I am a decent one. Mr. P's affection for his (robotic) hospice cat opened a window to the impact of love and nurture on an increasingly opened heart and shrinkingly declining mind. And most of all, I hear the continued gratefulness for another day, another moment, another meal, another interaction, another trip, another summer or winter holiday, another family visit. Life's preciousness is not one to be taken for granted.

32. Chittick, *Sufism*, 56–57.

33. Chittick, *Sufism*, 88–102.

How the Elders Helped Shape My Pastoral Heart

My perpetual worry when I first started interning as a chaplain was if I had the right being there. Women as Islamic religious authority have two faces: she is either an *ustadha*, a literal religious teacher that teaches religion and/or Quran recitation, or she is a scholar who has earned either her traditional Islamic science *ijazah*, or scholarly licenses, or a post-doctorate in Islamic studies. I am neither. Throughout my training, I received an abundance of lovingkindness, mentorship, and pouring of stories of women clergy trailblazers that gave me the humble confidence I could take up the mantle too. The practice of chaplaincy expanded my own resonance of living life religiously through being grounded spiritually, interpersonally. Being my Muslim self while extending spiritual care to the elders and their caregivers has been a wonderment of water ripples:

> There's a ripple effect in all we do—
> What you do, touches me;
> What I do, touches you. (author unknown)[34]

Growing up personally and professionally under the eyes of so many older adults has been the most affirming practice of care I have been gifted. My heart has been nurtured under the guidance of so many sages in these older adults, likely unbeknownst to them of their perpetual impact. The heart I carry not only is an intentional spiritual caregiver, God willing, but also a mindful educator, a conscientious and loving mother, loving wife, daughter, friend, sister, neighbor.

ELDERLY CARE IN ISLAM: DOES SENIOR LIVING COMMUNITY MEAN NEGLECTING RESPONSIBILITIES?

In closing, and returning to the cultural and religious notions of the rights of elders to be cared for in Islam, perhaps the Islamic construct of *birr al-wālidayn*—being dutiful to one's parents—can be understood less as an over-functioning mandate that children must do everything, and more as an ethic of care that can be shared. From my single personal experience, there is a rich practice of planned senior living communities that can sustain the rights of the elders to be cared for warmly, ethically, appropriately by a community of caregivers, outside and alongside family members.

34. Way Foundation, "Way Foundation."

There are also the unspoken expectations within Islamic teachings on elderly care that leave little room for factual hardships many children caregivers bear. While heaven is said to be under the feet of mothers, I have sat with many whose mothers and fathers were unable to live up to such a pedigree of Godly honor. The assumption that *sabr* (patience) and respect for elders require children caregivers to surrender their agency and meet every demand ignores the real complexities of caregiving. Conflating respect to diminishing of self has been culturally how I myself have experienced my own community and family engagement in elderly care. Perhaps extending the practice of mutuality into the Islamic perspective of elderly care can be a starting point in reengaging the hadith and Quranic tradition on the topic. Starting with context rather than ideal theology revitalizes the lived theology we all swirl in. I wonder, starting with context, how would the following Quranic verse be reengaged?

> Thy Lord decrees that you worship none but Him, and be virtuous to parents. Whether one of both of them reaches old age, say not to them "Uff!" nor chide them, but speak unto them a noble word. Lower unto them the wing of humility out of mercy and say, "My Lord! Have mercy upon them, as they raised me when I was small."[35]

In my own humble interpretation from a trauma lens of human experience, this verse does not negate the discord one may feel toward their parents, nor disallow expressions of exasperation—in healthy ways. When the verse invites us to speak to parents with honor and kindness, reading it through lived experience opens an opportunity for one to recognize when they cannot engage their elderly parents without being triggered. I also hear in these verses what integration aspiration could look like:

1. The acknowledgment of the human experience to want to say "uff!" when dealing with parents including elderly ones;
2. To recognize in oneself when boundaries need to be erected, and to pause and restabilize one's emotions before further engagement;
3. To take the opportunity always and forevermore in both good and challenging times to submit to the will of God, and to seek God's help particularly in challenging times;

35. Nasr, *Study Quran* 17:23–24.

4. The acknowledgment that dealing with elderly, aging parents is challenging.

Giving myself the permission to reread these verses from a perspective of mutuality gives me a little more breathing room to be my most Muslim self without the shame and immense guilt of missing being an ideal one. Perhaps when Muslims can reengage in our notions of elderly care, it need not leave us to only have guilt in not doing our absolute best for our aging parents. And that perhaps could include imagining Muslim older adults living in senior living communities.

CONCLUSION

Providing an Islamic perspective on elderly care in the beginning felt monumental. I initially wrote this essay solely from the Islamic perspective on elderly care, meaning leaving myself out and merely giving historical and scholarly context on the topic. As I continue to grow not only in my pastoral heart and identity, but also in my spiritual care practice and education, I was able to shift toward the notion that I could be one Islamic perspective on elderly care. The gift of being Muslim is my own openness to wisdom wherever she originates. I am endlessly gifted by those I walk amongst daily. And having received much of elderly illumination, I hope this essay can be seen as my own giving back to the elderly community that is so dear to me.

BIBLIOGRAPHY

Al-Heeti, Roaa M. "Why Nursing Homes Will Not Work: Caring for the Needs of the Aging Muslim American Population." *The Elder Law Journal* 15 (2007) 206–31.

Chittick, William C. *Sufism: A Beginner's Guide*. Oxford: Oneworld, 2000.

———. *Me and Rumi: The Autobiography of Shams-I Tabrizi*. Translated by William Chittick. Louisville: Fons Vitae, 2004.

Clemetson, Lynette. "U.S. Muslims Confront Taboo on Nursing Homes." *The New York Times*, June 13, 2006.

Espinoza, Robert. "Immigrant and the Direct Care Workforce." PHI, June 2017. https://www.phinational.org/wp-content/uploads/2017/06/immigrants_and_the_direct_care_workforce_-_phi_-_june_2017.pdf.

Feil, Naomi, and Vicki de Klerk-Rubin. *Validation Breakthrough: Simple Techniques for Communicating with People with Alzheimer's and Other Dementias*. 4th ed. Baltimore, MD: Health Profession, 2022.

Fitzgerald, Edward. *Rubáiyát of Omar Khayyám*. Edited by Daniel Karlin. Oxford: Oxford University Press, 2009.

Nasr, Seyyed Hossein, et al., eds. *The Study Quran: A New Translation and Commentary*. New York: HarperCollins, 2015.
US Department of Labor. "The Essential Workers of the Coronavirus Pandemic." https://www.dol.gov/general/aboutdol/hallofhonor/2022-essential-workers.
Way Foundation. "Way Foundation." https://www.wayfoundationfamily.org.

5

From the Valley to the Open Plain

Reflections on the Role of Executive Officer for Mission and Ministry at Saint Francis Ministries, a Faith-Based Child and Family Welfare Agency

THE REVEREND ANDREW T. O'CONNOR

Religion that is pure and undefiled before God, the Father, is this: to care for orphans and widows in their distress. (Jas 1:27 NRSV)

In the fall of 2022, I was working in my office in the parish in which I then served as rector when I received a message from a friend and colleague (and our diocese's canon to the ordinary) that Saint Francis Ministries was looking to hire an Episcopal priest to serve as the organization's first-ever executive officer for Mission and Ministry, and that this person would be based in Wichita, Kansas. At the time, I was more focused on the exciting possibility of having a new non-parochial priestly colleague join us in Wichita than I was on the job description that my friend had forwarded. Little did I know that in the coming weeks I would be asked by two other friends involved with the organization to consider putting my name in for the position. As the late fall turned to winter and then spring and successive rounds of interviews gave way to the substantive conversations that would lead me to join Saint Francis Ministries, I came to realize that I was the non-parochial priest I and my other Wichita Episcopal colleagues had been hoping for! God indeed works in mysterious ways that often confound and yet delight us—not least of which are the career plans we think we have engineered for ourselves. What follows is a reflection on this new role and its place within a major Episcopal-Church-affiliated child and family welfare agency, and what might be useful for the current conversations about the future of ministry in a rapidly changing church and world.

Saint Francis Ministries was founded in 1945 by the Reverend Robert H. Mize Jr., an Episcopal priest assigned to a preaching circuit in a large swath of western Kansas, as a home for boys who had no other place to go in the Depression, World War II, and post-War years. Fr. Bob, as he was always known, had noticed throughout his travels around the geography of his assigned ministry area that there were a high number of preteen and teenage boys who had become separated for various reasons from their families. These adolescents were in routine trouble with the local authorities, and many were experiencing some form of abandonment and homelessness. Fr. Bob was convinced that there had to be a better way forward for these young men than perpetual entanglement with the law. His conviction led him to take the necessary steps to purchase the abandoned county poor farm in Ellsworth, Kansas, and to establish the first Saint Francis Home for Boys. This remarkable story is chronicled in Emily Gardiner Neal's 1963 biography *Father Bob and His Boys.*

Initially facing several challenges from the local community over the home and his idea that there was a compassionate approach to rehabilitating these young men who had been wandering the highways and byways of rural Kansas, Fr. Bob's initial success quickly led to the founding of a second home. The key to Fr. Bob's approach was the concept of offering the homes as a place where the boys in his care would experience unconditional love; experience forgiveness as the primary instrument of transformation; learn to be honest about and accountable for their actions; live in the least-restrictive setting possible that would allow them to receive the benefits of an education, and to begin and end each day with God. Fr. Bob termed this approach "therapy in Christ," and believed that it was the formula for making a difference in the lives of the boys who would come to Saint Francis. The people who initially doubted or feared this experiment in the practical application of the gospel imperative to love the least and lost were eventually won over by the transformation they experienced firsthand in the boys' lives. So-called "juvenile delinquents" were being restored to their families, friends, and the wider community in a way that truly appeared miraculous.

Behind every such miracle, however, is something a little more nuanced and complex. Fr. Bob had a clear vision for what he hoped to achieve in the transformation of the lives of the young men he encountered in western Kansas. He relied profoundly on his faith but also his persuasive talents to tell a compelling story about what God was doing in a part of the country that is often overlooked and underappreciated. The challenges he would face were not unlike the challenges faced by any founder of a new mission or ministry seeking to renew the gospel call to service: fear, doubt, misunderstanding, opportunism, and, of course, funding challenges! But he was also able to inspire folks with his vision and to build a team who would help him establish Saint Francis Ministries for the long-term and as a force for good across nearly eight decades. He also had the wisdom to step away from the work after fifteen years (having been appointed as a bishop in what is now Namibia), allowing successive generations of leaders to take forward the collective vision of transforming lives through the power of Christ's unfailing love.

The decade-by-decade story of the growth and transformation of that first boys' home in Ellsworth to the multifaceted child and family welfare agency working in seven states that is the present-day Saint Francis Ministries (SFM) is both worthy of being told and beyond the present scope of this work. However, before turning to a consideration of the role and purpose of the executive officer for Mission and Ministry (EOMM) within this organization and what might be learned from it with respect to the growing fields of chaplaincy and sector-ministries, it must be noted that that transformation was affected by subsequent generations of dedicated leaders, both ordained and lay. The child welfare professionals who were attracted to and advanced the reach of SFM over the years—such as former Chief Clinical Officer Cheryl Rathbun, who was with SFM for forty-five years, and Special Assistant to the President and former Chief Program Officer Trish Bryant, who will have been with SFM for thirty-nine years when she retires in June 2024—fairly uniformly describe their work in the terms of a vocation. Understanding this sense of calling, and the attendant feelings of commitment and belonging it engenders in the organization, is the crucial context for understanding the crisis that occurred in 2020 that ultimately lead to the creation of the EOMM position.

The precondition for understanding the role of the EOMM position at SFM, and thus what such a role might suggest for chaplaincy and sector ministries in general, is a detour away from the generally positive story of

Fr. Bob and the leaders who followed him to a much more difficult period of the organization's history. In 2020, a whistleblower complaint revealed evidence of misconduct sufficient to result in the termination of SFM's executive leadership. The time immediately following these events and lasting approximately eighteen months thereafter are known colloquially within SFM as "The Valley," as in "the valley of the shadow of death" of Ps 23. Because SFM is a faith-based entity with a deep historic tie to the Episcopal Church, the use of religious language to describe this part of the organization's recent history may seem a little too on the nose. But it is a helpful compass point by which to orient the path charted through that difficult time to the present moment under consideration.

The Valley presented SFM with such challenges that it is not an exaggeration to describe that time as an existential threat to the whole organization. Were SFM to have ceased operations, the impact would have been felt keenly by the nearly 12,000 children and families the organization serves annually. Beyond the provision of services to our clients, the closure of SFM would have also resulted in job losses for nearly 1,700 employees working across the six states that then made up the organization's footprint. The team of leaders, at both the operational and board governance levels, that stepped up to meet that eighteen-month moment must be commended for their courage and commitment to save SFM so that it could continue its vital mission. In particular, the leadership of Interim President and CEO William Clark was essential in bringing SFM through The Valley. A committed Christian and a retired US Army colonel, Bill Clark brought his experience in large and complex organizations to bear on bringing SFM back to its three primary competencies: out-of-home foster care services, residential care, and prevention services. This return to core competencies meant some painful, and at times quite public, movement away from work initiated under former leadership. Bill Clark's success at building and empowering a truly remarkable team of senior executive leaders—Lora Winchell, Cristian Garcia, John McDowell, Ray Nunweiler, John Thurston, and Amanda Pfannenstiel, as well as the previously mentioned Trish Bryant and Cheryl Rathbun—who renewed and focused SFM's mission and vision resulted in his being named the seventh president and CEO, removing the interim tag. Of note, this means Colonel Clark is the first lay and the first non-Episcopalian president to lead Saint Francis Ministries.

In the period of stabilization following the successful navigation of the immediate crisis of The Valley, one might suppose that a reevaluation of

SFM's historic affiliation with the Episcopal Church would likely result in a distancing between the organization and the Church, but this would prove not to be the case! Certainly, conversations took place across the organization about whether and how that connection might continue. This conversation, prompted by what many internal and external stakeholders felt was a profound betrayal by the former leadership, ultimately determined that being a faith-based organization was an essential component of SFM's identity. Considering such complex questions requires thoughtful leadership willing to entertain difficult interpretations of the stories that have always been told in an organization alongside the stories being told in the wake of a crisis—not least of which are taking place in public forums like local and national media. Additionally, these questions must be asked and answered with reference not only to the ecclesiastical but also the civil and legal structures that guide and govern independent, nonprofit organizations. Beyond the philosophical quandaries involved in parsing Episcopal identity in an organization in the twenty-first century, there are significant practical realities that cannot be ignored. Chief among these for an organization engaged in child and family welfare work is that the absolute majority of SFM's funding comes from state grants and contracts. Public money does not prohibit SFM from being a faith-based organization, but it does mean the work is directed for the universal public good rather than a specific ecclesial outcome. In other words, though SFM is guided by its religious values, it is not a church.

What then would the role of a confident, yet appropriately humble, Episcopal identity be in an SFM that had weathered the trial and tribulation of The Valley? How could that identity be a strength rather than a liability, especially in a rapidly changing, post-pandemic child and family welfare landscape? How might a renewed Episcopal identity not only benefit SFM but be an opportunity for the Episcopal Church to reengage with work that aligns with its mission of bearing good news, binding up the brokenhearted, and being a light in the darkness? The answers to these questions are being crafted in real time and are grounded in a dynamic framework of call and response, a framework of vocation. I believe that having entered, traveled through, and exited The Valley, Saint Francis Ministries has come to a period that might be called "The Open Plain."

A key image in the Hebrew Scriptures is the open plain, or good and broad land, that God promises to Abraham and his descendants. The covenant relationship that God establishes with Abraham, Isaac, and Jacob as described in the book of Genesis is predicated on a vital exchange of obedience to God in worship on the part of the chosen human actors for the opportunity to flourish in a specific place. The good and broad land that God promises is not merely an internal state of contentment but an actual place for God's people to reside. This special place has specific features that demonstrate God's desire to bless God's people. In Exodus, this land is described as "full with milk and honey" (Exod 3:18 CEB). By the time of Israel's gaining possession of the promised land, God's people have wandered near and far; they have experienced oppression in Egypt and God's mighty work of liberation. While God's people wandered in the wilderness after Egypt, they were being prepared for entry into this land that would fulfill God's promise. This physical journey certainly had spiritual ramifications but that makes it no less a physical journey. The Hebrew Scriptures are clear that this journey was a logistical undertaking marked by specific instructions for the construction of the tabernacle and the arrangement of the Hebrews' camps. The open plain that the children of Israel enter is a material reality that suggests important spiritual truths that extend beyond a particular point in history. The open plain represents an ideal relationship between God and God's people that is grounded in a lived experience of time and place. It is grounded in, well, the ground! Following a period of deep difficulty, whether slavery in Egypt or the nearly catastrophic collapse of an organization, the horizon of an open plain as a real place where healing occurs, and hope is restored, is a profoundly welcoming sight.

Taking into consideration the long-term and more recent history of SFM, the challenges of the child and family welfare sector, and the forces that are shaping life in the first quarter of the twenty-first century, The Open Plain is nothing other than a time of remarkable opportunity for this organization. Not only is this true for SFM, but I believe it is true for the church universal and for every society and culture present in God's creation. This is a bold claim, but the Spirit is constantly moving ordinary people to do surprisingly audacious things. Thus, in an organization like SFM which works with some of the most vulnerable people in our society—children in the foster care system, families facing significant behavioral and mental health struggles, adults with intellectual and developmental disabilities—our most significant asset is our frontline workers. These members of the SFM team daily come alongside people facing some of the most difficult, trauma-induced challenges. To rise to this work, I assert that people need to understand what they are doing as a calling. While I am not inclined to impose my own theological framework on the unwilling, I would nevertheless further specify that this calling comes from God—and that God will supply the grace necessary to answer it. The calling comes from God, and it expects a response in the form of our action on behalf of the vulnerable. This is what it means today, at SFM, to guide our journey towards The Open Plain as a place of renewed encounter with God and revealed purpose in accepting the vocation of a redeemed humanity.

Understood in the light of the scriptural image of The Open Plain as a real place where the divine is encountered in the work of serving those in need, moving beyond the real place of challenge that was The Valley thanks to skillful and committed leadership, returning to but also expanding upon the rich history of our Episcopal identity, the potential inherent in the role of executive officer for Mission and Ministry is taking shape. To be sure, and to borrow a phrase from Wichita's history as a primary center for the aviation industry, it can feel like the work of the EOMM is "flying the plane while building it." As singular as this role is in a unique organization, I believe that it provides an important template for consideration in the shaping of similar ministries that take place outside of the traditional ecclesial sphere. I also believe that it may have something meaningful to offer for those whose ministries take place in the usual parochial settings.

A narrative review, based on the original position description used to recruit the first EOMM, will be helpful in teasing out the implications for chaplaincy and other sector ministry roles. Fundamentally, the EOMM helps to shape, grow, and sustain the spiritual commitments of Saint Francis Ministries. The EOMM serves as a chief officer of the organization alongside the other chief officers who comprise the senior leadership team. While being an integral part of that senior leadership team, a particular gift that the EOMM brings to this work is one of availability across all the organization's programs and its extensive geographical footprint (twenty-seven program locations in Kansas, Nebraska, Oklahoma, Texas, Arkansas, Mississippi, and soon to be Ohio). As an Episcopal priest, the EOMM is SFM's chief clerical/ordained representative to the Episcopal Church and other ecumenical partners. The work of the EOMM is by necessity collaborative with senior leaders, board members, and staff at every level. At the time of this writing, the Mission and Ministry department of SFM is exactly one person, the EOMM!

The primary work of the EOMM role is to steward the soul, spirit, and values of SFM in collaboration with a diverse and inclusive leadership team, workforce, and client base. The EOMM is called to model a missional form of leadership with a genuine and interactive confidence in spirituality for the health and wellbeing of the whole organization and those it serves. In order to accomplish this broad task, the EOMM is committed to the growth of sustainable spiritual practices through SFM. Additionally, the EOMM provides pastoral support, both collectively and individually, for SFM in times of change, challenge, or trauma. As previously indicated, the EOMM seeks to renew and enhance engagement with the wider Episcopal Church, church partners in all denominations, and other partners of good faith who are aligned with SFM's mission. The EOMM also has a public-facing role as an advocate for children, families, and IDD adults in the wider community—this often takes the form of preaching in local congregations; serving on the board of a local, faith-based, justice-focused community organization; addressing legislators and political advocacy groups; or offering the benediction at community events. The purpose of the EOMM position is to align the mission, vision, and values of SFM as a faith-based, nonprofit social service agency dedicated to the welfare of children and families. Mission and Ministry at SFM is established for joyfully answering God's call to raise up leaders who serve the most vulnerable members of our communities with unconditional love and transformative grace after the manner of our Lord Jesus Christ.

The practical form of this work falls primarily into three areas (what we at SFM colloquially call "buckets"): missional leadership, church and community engagement, and collaborative resource development. When originally framing out these buckets and the essential functions in each one during the first several months in this role, it became clear that there was a welcome and necessary overlap that linked and directed the work. An operational plan was developed to define these areas and assign priorities, tasks, and cadences to each. Just as we have a living faith and a living history at SFM, that operational plan continues as a living document that is open to regular review and refinement over time, with input from the CEO, other senior leaders, and the SFM board. The purpose of the operational plan is to put into "time and space" the work of serving all our SFM people as the EOMM bears witness to the redemptive power of Jesus Christ's life, death, and rising to life again. The theological through line for all that has been described is that the EOMM is primarily a role of witness expressed in shared leadership, relationship building, and the stewarding of spiritual resources for mission.

What are the essential daily functions of the EOMM at SFM? The first and perhaps most important function of the EOMM is to pray. The EOMM prays daily for the organization, stakeholders, partners, and the foster care community at large. This takes place in the personal prayer of the EOMM (in my recitation of the Daily Office) and in various public ways such as at the start of meetings, company-wide and program-specific town halls, and ceremonies such as retirements or National Adoption Day. The EOMM also monitors the prayer requests that come in from the SFM website, praying for intentions that come in from around the world, and interacting with those who have requested prayer. The importance of prayer as a function of the EOMM position ties back directly to Fr. Bob Mize's contention that every day at SFM begins and ends with God. This is the important centering context for the missional leadership bucket and informs all the work of the EOMM as a senior executive working with the other chief officers and senior leaders.

The EOMM is also responsible for producing a daily devotional email that is sent company-wide and serves as an example of an encouragement towards a lively spirituality in the organization. Topics for this reflection have included Scripture verses, saints' days, liturgical seasons, spiritual wisdom from ecumenical sources, and all with a focus on the unique calling of child and family welfare work and with reference to the challenges and joys of such work. Themes for writing are often suggested by events impacting the organization or in conjunction with various leadership initiatives. Themes surface from interaction with members of the SFM workforce. Most days, the EOMM will receive responses to the daily devotional from SFM team members indicating gratitude for connecting spirituality to their lived experience of the work. These interactions provide a potential jumping-off point for pastoral care if needed. The EOMM produces public-facing blog posts and other occasional messaging through internal communications platforms. The EOMM is working with members of the SFM Marketing and Communications team to further develop ways to expand internal and external spiritual messaging; examples under consideration include podcasts, videos, and a livestreamed or recorded weekly sermon. The EOMM has also made a handful of media appearances on *Good Day Kansas*, supported by the Marketing and Communications team, to promote the spiritual dimensions of child and family welfare work.

The provision of a program of regular worship is an area under consideration by the EOMM but has yet to be determined due to the unique challenge of having a large geographic footprint, a hybrid workforce, and only one EOMM! Several team members, especially those with a long history of working at SFM, have fond memories of chapel services being held—particularly at the residential campuses which all have chapels and when the organization employed more clergy—and have requested some form of worship to be reinstated. Worship has been coordinated by the EOMM for two board retreats, drawing on the riches of *The Book of Common Prayer* and Anglican tradition. Additionally, Ashes To Go was offered by the EOMM at one location, by request of local leadership, for Ash Wednesday, and was well received. More opportunities for worship, both for the workforce and for those in our care, especially at residential locations, is an area of potential growth in the organization.

The EOMM can also be described as providing a ministry of presence. This normally takes the form of visits to SFM offices and with various teams, as well as "office hours" for those who request a meeting. Pastoral care work often takes place in the form of trauma debriefs. These sessions can be requested by a team supervisor or program director when team members have been involved with a traumatic event in the course of their work. Any traumatic event could warrant this request, but often they are related to an exposure to violence or the death of a client, staff member, or another provider partner. These debriefs are trauma-informed sessions intended to help team members process what has happened, to reassure that what they may be experiencing is a natural outcome of primary or secondary trauma, and to reinforce the resources available through the organization and in the team members' own communities of care.

This ministry of presence also overlaps with the bucket of church and community engagement in that the EOMM is the primary point of contact with the Episcopal Church, partner churches in all denominations, other faith-based nonprofits, and other community-focused organizations with which SFM partners to accomplish our mission to children, families, and IDD adults. The EOMM is encouraged and expected to preach, teach, and supply in Episcopal churches, especially those within the geographic footprint of SFM. This allows the EOMM to share the good news of how SFM ministers in the name of all Episcopalians and to renew and refresh connections with the church. For instance, the EOMM stands ready to address an outreach committee or help connect a congregation with a program in need of support. This form of engagement is envisioned as helping individuals, groups, and parishes put faith into action. This work of engagement is not limited to the Episcopal Church, as SFM has partnerships with communities of faith across the ecumenical spectrum. An area of opportunity for the EOMM is connecting with community-based ministerial alliances, colleague groups, and other professional networks of clergy and religious leaders, especially in communities where we have a significant presence. The goal is to become the "go-to" person for such organizations or individuals to consult with on matters relating to faith and child and family welfare. Moreover, the development of these connections would also help raise awareness in communities that struggle with capacity issues that impact service delivery for children in care. Regular meetings with assorted denominational leaders (bishops, superintendents, ministers general, etc.) are another opportunity to connect the wider religious community with the work of SFM. Reaching out to various Episcopal Church religious orders is also bearing some early fruit in developing a network of partnership and prayer.

The final bucket of collaborative resource development has the EOMM attending to the development of resources—both financial and spiritual—that help to advance the mission and vision of SFM. This work is collaborative as it involves both the operational and fiduciary/governance functions of the EOMM who is both a senior executive leader and an *ex officio* member of the SFM Board (with voice, but not vote). In this way, the collaborative resource development bucket overlaps the missional leadership bucket. The EOMM supports the work of the philanthropic arm of SFM, the Saint Francis Foundation, and helps bridge the foundation's work with that of the Marketing and Communications team. The heart of this work is telling the story of SFM in compelling ways, highlighting our successes and inviting deeper partnership. In this way, the collaborative resource development bucket overlaps the church and community engagement bucket. A good recent example of how these different buckets work together has been the presence of the EOMM as an exhibitor and participant at two diocesan conventions and at the annual conference of the Episcopal Parish Network. Also, and this is critical, the EOMM is a major proponent of sending handwritten thank-you notes to individual donors, donor churches, and other donor organizations to incarnate the gratitude that our organization has for those who support our work with children and families!

The executive officer for Mission and Ministry is a unique position in a unique Episcopal-Church-affiliated organization. It is not a pure chaplain role—though I believe a study of the work of command-level military chaplains might prove useful in the continuing development of the role. Nor is it a purely administrative or executive role as it carries significant spiritual responsibilities. It is also not an exact parallel to a traditional rector position, though it similarly includes spiritual and administrative duties. I suspect it might be related to mission and ministry positions in religious university or seminary settings but, again, with enough difference based on the populations it serves. What I can say for certain about it, though, is that it provides a distinct opportunity for a deep engagement with the movements of God's Spirit in an organization that understands itself to be doing the hands-on work of the gospel. The unique calling of this organization across its rich history, through periods of growth and existential challenge, is to help people move from their own valleys into the open plains of God's blessing. As the church continues to rapidly change, opportunities for those preparing for ordained and lay leadership to consider forms of ministry such as this, or other entrepreneurial ventures infused by the same spirit as our founder Fr. Bob Mize, should be explored and encouraged. Answering this call as the executive officer for Mission and Ministry has not only helped me help others put their faith into action but expanded my own sense of vocation as an Episcopal priest and as a baptized Christian.

6

School Chaplaincy

A Seed Worth Planting

THE REV. ELIZABETH REES

INTRODUCTION

In my Scripture classes with high schoolers, when we talk about parables, I always start with the parable of the mustard seed from Matthew's Gospel:

> [Jesus] put before the disciples another parable: "The kingdom of heaven is like a mustard seed that someone took and sowed in his field; it is the smallest of all the seeds, but when it has grown it is the greatest of shrubs and becomes a tree, so that the birds of the air come and make nests in its branches." (Matt 13:31–32 NRSVue)

I find that there's something about the simplicity and vividness of that story that invites my students to engage. It doesn't seem overly detailed or complicated to them, so they aren't afraid to offer their own interpretations, the way they sometimes are with Scripture.

We start with a group practice of modified *Lectio Divina*, reading the passage three times with a different prompt for each:

1. Listen for a word or phrase that stands out for you.
2. What does this word or phrase make you wonder or think about? What does it make you feel?

3. What do you think you can learn from this word or phrase? What might it have to do with you today?

After each reading, we sit in silence briefly (with the opportunity to journal if they'd like), and then we go around the room and share our responses to the prompts. And maybe because it feels like a children's story rather than an imposing Scripture passage, it seems to come alive for the students as they draw forth connections to the story. They may not see it as having anything to do with God, but they can read meaning into it that has something to do with their lives. Some find themselves in the idea that something seen as inconsequential or worthless by most of the world has great underlying potential or find hope in the thought that it may take time to see tangible results from the work they do. Others talk about gratitude for the small moments in their own lives, and the inner beauty and value of things that we tend to look past. Sometimes they name their own experience of a place that makes them feel safe and comfortable. Or they may rejoice in (and long for) a world where a diverse group can truly belong.

As the students notice details and wonder about this parable, they get a glimpse of the depth and relevance of Scripture, and have an experience of listening and learning from each other. Only after they've entered into the parable for themselves do I introduce them to the background and historical context of the passage. That no self-respecting farmer would ever intentionally plant mustard in their field. That this parable would have served as encouragement for early disciples in their darkest days. That this parable may have served as a nod to the broadening scope of Jesus's message—what had once been thought to be just for a certain family, or a certain tribe, or a certain religion, was slowly but surely broadening in scope. The relative safety of the mustard seed parable serves as a starting place that gives the class a foundation for jumping into the opportunity and challenge of Scripture.

Maybe it's because I've returned to it so many times and heard so many thoughtful responses to it from my students that this parable has become a sort of guiding metaphor for the work that I'm doing in the world of school chaplaincy.

There are endless parallels between school ministry and Jesus's deceptively short and simple story: How do we chaplains sow what we have to offer intentionally and faithfully in our schools, and continue joyfully even when the "soil" is hostile or disinterested? How do we patiently wait for growth, or even become comfortable holding lightly any certainty of tangible results? How do we notice and appreciate unintentional growth, or growth that may fall outside the usual margins of "success?" How do we invite and welcome "all the birds of the air" to find belonging and make their homes in our schools?

If there ever was a ministry where challenges abound, school chaplaincy is it. And yet, those challenges are completely intertwined with opportunities. In this day and age where church attendance is consistently declining, school chaplains have full congregations in every chapel service, a proverbial mission field of largely unchurched people. But the truth is, those "congregations" are largely there only because they have to be.

At a time when the church struggles to prove its importance to people for whom tradition is immaterial and the Bible a dusty and irrelevant document, chaplains have a chance to introduce Scripture to "spiritual but not religious" young people who are often seen as the so-called "future of the church," and to acquaint them with the Bible's call for justice in an ancient context that looks surprisingly similar to our own. But those classes are also a constant and tricky balance of academic rigor and relationship, and their preparation leaves little time for everything else.

In a world where the church is being forced to rethink how to exist beyond its own walls, school chaplains have an opportunity to do ministry right where people are—in the school itself, in outside activities, and with the surrounding community. But chaplains also can find themselves struggling to integrate into a system that for the most part doesn't understand the role of a chaplain.

As William Temple, one-time archbishop of Canterbury in the Anglican Church and ecumenical leader, is attributed as saying, the church exists primarily for people that are not currently members. I think that is the glorious and unlikely promise of the mustard seed, with its surprising presence and its shocking growth and its open hospitality—all in service to the birds of the air. And that is also what school chaplains, at their best, can offer the communities they serve.

All that said, of course school chaplaincies are not all built alike. Some school chaplains will spend most of their time as a priest in an affiliated church and overlap with a school primarily for chapel and governance or logistical meetings. Others will be situated in boarding schools where their duties extend to coaching sports teams and living on campus with evening and weekend dorm duties. Some spend most of their time teaching, and others are primarily pastors or priests. Some are solo chaplains, and others are part of large chaplaincy teams. And, of course, chaplains find themselves situated at schools with students of many different faiths and with varying emphases on evangelism. All of these factors will affect the chaplaincy experience and expectations.

My particular context is St. Stephens and St. Agnes School (SSSAS), where I serve as senior chaplain. As our self-description in admission and marketing materials puts it, SSSAS is a "co-ed college preparatory Episcopal Church School in Alexandria, Virginia that educates students from ages three through grade twelve." SSSAS is one of six member schools of the Church Schools in the Episcopal Diocese of Virginia, with about 1,200 students. SSSAS is located six miles from Washington, DC, and draws students from Maryland, Northern Virginia, and DC. The school has three distinct campuses (lower, middle, and upper schools) that are not within walking distance. While the three divisions share connections through academic departments, administrative oversight, and periodic all-school and all-faculty gatherings, on a daily logistical basis, they function largely separately.

Our chaplain team comprises four priests, with two based on the upper school campus and one each on the Lower and middle school campuses. Chaplains teach at least a 75-percent load of classes, lead one weekly chapel service for their division, provide pastoral care for students and faculty, and collaborate with the administrative leaders on their campuses in their hybrid faculty/administrator roles.

All schools are different, which means that no two chaplaincies will look the same. But one thing will probably be the same in all school ministry settings—the chaplain will have multiple overlapping (and sometimes overwhelming) roles that create both countless challenges and limitless opportunities, much like branches of a giant mustard tree.

WORSHIP

At least on the surface, the thing that most clearly distinguishes a religious school from a secular school is common worship. At many schools, worship is one of the few times the community regularly comes together, and, for the most part, it is a time that is valued, even by the reluctant or nonreligious. The frequency of worship varies widely among schools. Some schools offer daily chapel services, and others gather only once a week. And often worship is truncated from the norm in a church setting, necessitating that liturgical priorities be made by the chaplain. At my school, chapel services are about thirty minutes once a week, and slightly longer for our periodic celebrations of Eucharist. (If I could change one thing about my school to strengthen our religious identity, it would be to increase our worship services to twice a week.) There is also a great variety in the religiosity of school worship. Some schools' chapel services closely mirror their religion or denomination's usual worship practices, and others might feel more like nonreligious assemblies or interfaith gatherings.

While my school highly values hospitality and seeks to make our liturgy understandable and our hymns singable, our prayers, readings, music, and Eucharistic celebrations are unapologetically Christian in focus. Although we might give special attention to a theme that connects to the world (like Black History Month, for instance) or acknowledge and hold in our prayers the parallel religious observances of our interfaith brothers and sisters, our worship at SSSAS is Episcopalian in feel. Our chapels tend to be flexible as to lectionary readings, but regularly celebrate and teach about the liturgical seasons and holy days that fall during the school year.

However, chaplain colleagues in different schools (whether Episcopal or other varieties of denomination or religion) report a range of chapel experience. Some hew strictly to their denominations' practices, and others invite liturgical leadership from multiple faith groups or focus on secular themes to celebrate in chapel. (I attended a conference where a chaplain at a Christian school said they were discouraged from mentioning Jesus or singing religious hymns in chapel, and were not planning to celebrate Easter in worship.)

Because of the wide variation, it is important for a potential chaplain to get a clear sense of a school's worship norms, and to discern whether they are comfortable with whatever that norm is (or comfortable fighting against the current to achieve what they'd hope to see) before assuming the role. Space may also be an issue. While some schools have religious spaces that are set aside only for that purpose, others worship in multipurpose spaces. Our chapel services at SSSAS take part in shared spaces, which require clearer communication and more intensive setup than would a traditional liturgical setting. Our Lower and middle school chapels take place in gyms, difficult to beautify, and requiring that chairs and liturgical furniture be moved every week. The upper school chapel shares the performing arts space, so it is in a theater that by its nature inspires a subconscious expectation of "performance" rather than participation. Shared space can be tricky for logistics and relationships, and the spaces usually lack sacristies and ample storage.

The plus side of less traditional settings, and maybe of school worship in general, is that expectations for how chapel should look tend to be less cemented, allowing for more innovation. Our chaplain team at SSSAS lives into that possibility, using slides, music, and movement to form chapel services that are more creative, interactive, and age-appropriate than the average church service. For example, for our Christmas Lessons and Carols service on the upper school campus, we included short video clips of students answering questions related to the Scripture readings (e.g., "What would *you* do if an angel visited you?") and invited our seniors to spread out around the space with candles (battery-operated for safety) while strobe lights flashed during a reading of John's cosmic Christmas story. Because our chapel service isn't seen as "the principle Sunday service" of a parish, we have flexibility to lean into hospitality and inclusivity in our liturgy. We hope that our locations also serve as a reminder that God can be found anywhere and at all times, not only in sanctified spaces.

Schools are also uniquely positioned to show the inclusive and welcoming personality of God through student leadership and participation. Our lower school invites different grade levels to different tasks each week, depending on ability. Students take roles reading Scripture, leading psalms and prayers, and acolyting. Along with our chaplain, many faculty members of diverse backgrounds and traditions offer homilies for chapel. Parents are invited to attend, and are excited to see their children involved, to celebrate monthly birthday prayers, and to attend monthly post-chapel coffees. At the middle school, there is a student chapel choir, and each advisory takes a turn with liturgical leadership and hospitality roles throughout the school year. Homilies are given by our chaplain and other faculty members, and sometimes by visiting upper school students. The upper school has both a student chapel choir leading congregational singing, and a student vestry rotating through roles as worship leader, lectors, acolytes, and lay Eucharistic ministers. Our vestry consists of about eighteen upper-class students that are invited based on expressed interest and engagement in religion classes. They are the primary worship leaders and readers for our weekly chapel services, and also take part in leadership and prayers as needed for all-school chapel services and special events. The vestry is an ecumenical group of students comfortable(ish!) with being seen as faith leaders in the school. Most of them are not Episcopalian, and a few opt out of communion due to their own religious traditions. The vestry meets twice a month for prayer, fellowship, and worship planning, and to bring student ideas and feedback to the chaplains. Once a year, they take part in an overnight vestry retreat, allowing more time for faith formation and idea sharing. As with all student groups, some participants are more committed than others, some are better speakers and leaders than others, and they are a busy group with sometimes conflicting participation in other activities on campus.

We also invite other student involvement in chapel. For instance, student musicians and musical groups can play music and sing anthems during chapel. But the most sought-after student involvement comes in the form of chapel talks by our seniors. Each year, seniors are invited to apply to speak during chapel. At the upper school, seniors provide the "sermon" for about twenty of our thirty-six chapel services. The other students love hearing their peers speak about their life stories and challenges. Upper school chaplains work closely with the seniors as they craft their talks. Although we require some connection between their talk and Scripture, as one might expect, the student talks tend to be less "religious" and Scripture-based than the chaplains' sermons. We try to preserve regular preaching time, especially on important religious days, for our chaplains, but for clergy used to regular preaching, it is definitely a diminished part of our ministry.

The liturgical work of chaplains can also extend beyond chapel services. They may be invited to offer prayers outside the weekly worship context, whether for faculty meetings, social gatherings of school families, or admission events. Chaplains may also be an important part of leadership for formal events like baccalaureate and graduation, and have sacramental duties for community weddings, funerals, and baptisms. All of these can be great opportunities to form connections and extend the role of the chaplain beyond the school walls.

WORSHIP OPPORTUNITIES AND CHALLENGES

Opportunities

1. The chance to repeatedly affirm that all students are welcome and loved, and that their grades, successes, and failures do not define them in the eyes of God.
2. The honor of serving and blessing such a diverse group of students and faculty.

3. The ability to try new and creative things in worship and see student enthusiasm in response.
4. The joy of working with young people who feel ownership over worship.

Challenges

1. Depending on staff and students that may or may not have any worship experience or understanding for musical accompaniment, audiovisual support, bulletin or slide creation, and space setup.
2. Older students can be very reluctant congregational singers. Finding songs that this diverse and often unchurched group of people want to sing sometimes feels like an impossible task.
3. Chapel time may not be seen as a given by faculty and administrators. You may have to proactively protect chapel time (or find creative ways to reschedule) when faced with awards assemblies, snow days, exam schedules, and secular celebrations.
4. Traditions can be incredibly strong in schools, and you may be surprised about what the administration assumes should be part of chapel.
5. Depending on the tradition of your school and frequency of student or outside speakers during chapel, you may find yourself not getting to preach as much as you'd like.

TEACHING

In the parish, teaching obviously would be included within the realm of Christian formation. In the school setting, religion classes are decidedly more academic in nature. As the National Association of Episcopal Schools, the standard setter for schools in my own tradition, puts it: "The religious studies curriculum of Episcopal schools is as fully rigorous as any other academic course."[1] However, from conversations with chaplain colleagues, it seems like the experience of most religion teachers is that our classes aren't usually taken as seriously, or expected by other faculty or students to be as rigorous, as other academic classes.

1. National Association of Episcopal Schools, "Principles of Good Practice."

At my school, Religion is its own academic department, and our department chair is a faculty member and not a chaplain, although all of our chaplains have strong teaching roles within the department. In many schools, the head chaplain is also the head of the religion department.

On our lower school campus, religion is one of the "specials," along with music and art. Every student in the lower school has religion class every six school days. For most of the grades, Godly Play, a Montessori-based method of telling stories, provides the structure for the religion classes. In fourth and fifth grades, students are introduced to biblical themes, moral decision-making, and world religions.

In middle school, all sixth and eighth graders take religion classes. In sixth grade, students focus on world religions (including a beloved all-day field trip to visit a mosque, a synagogue, and a church). Eighth grade centers around biblical studies and ethical leadership, encouraging students to see the Bible's relevance in contemporary society and in their lives.

In the upper school, students are required to take a semester-long biblical studies class (which most students take in their freshman year), two quarters of Ethics (one each during sophomore and senior year), and one elective religion class.

Many chaplains find themselves positioned as full-time or almost-full-time teachers with little previous teaching training or experience. For me, beginning as a school chaplain after twelve years of parish ministry, teaching was definitely my growing edge. Sustained teaching is far different than Sunday school or youth ministry, with their focus on food, games, and faith-building. Classroom management definitely isn't taught in seminary! And I've yet to find an existing curriculum that feels quite right.

Meanwhile, chaplains are constantly balancing their pastoral role with providing educational rigor in line with our academic colleagues. Chaplains differ in where they fall on the continuum between academic teaching and faith formation, and sometimes those choices can lead to tension with academic religion-teacher counterparts. For instance, I begin my classes with diverse opportunities for prayer and meditation, ranging from breath prayers to *Lectio Divina* (as mentioned above) to mandala creation, whereas some religion department colleagues see themselves as purely academic teachers. Like many non-core classes, religion offerings are sometimes viewed with skepticism and seen as unserious by other academic departments and college counselors. Our students, facing academic pressures to fill their schedules with as many high-level courses as possible, sometimes see religion classes as something to get through or get past, and expect "easy A's." Some religios schools for this reason have made religion classes pass-fail.

Substantively, our classes present challenges as well. With a short time to expose students to Scripture and religion, which pieces do we include and which do we leave out? How much attention do we pay to the ancient context and how much to application of Scripture in our own modern context? Should an ethics class focus on teaching about ethical principles and systems? Or is it our job to encourage ethical development and leadership in our students? Should we focus on Christian ethics or broaden outward and introduce even morally questionable systems? Are we Christian chaplains even qualified to teach something like world religions?

But despite the questions religion classes pose, they also present chaplains with sustained time to get to know students. We get a glimpse of where students are on their own journeys as we invite their wonder and exploration. Classes also engage in what in the Episcopal Church is widely affirmed—that faith and reason are intertwined, and that good questions are preferred over easy answers. In our diverse classrooms, we can invite and benefit from both the different perspectives and dedication to faith of our multi-faith brothers and sisters, and the credulous questions of atheists.

Opportunities

1. Hearing completely new perspectives on stories that might have become rote is great for your own creative reimagining.
2. Every class cycle is a chance to begin again if things don't feel like they are working, and teaching skills and confidence improve with each new class.
3. Preaching fodder abounds!

Challenges

1. Most students will not spare your feelings. If you are boring, they will let you know as they put their head on their desk, stare blankly, or respond with deadly silence.

2. Even the most experienced teachers seem to sometimes have a group of students that they just can't seem to engage. This can be very disheartening!
3. The siren song of technology is no joke. If you don't want students distracted, make sure computers are closed and phones are stored away at the start of class.

SPIRITUAL FORMATION AND PASTORAL CARE

Increasingly, religious schools find that fewer families are connected to a worship community. Sometimes that is an intentional choice, but often it is a product of increasing busyness and family commitments. More and more families in religious schools seem to consider their children's school to be their church, looking to schools not just for worship but also for faith formation and pastoral care.

Spiritual Formation

The prime opportunity for spiritual formation in a religious school is offered through chapel, but often the chaplain facilitates other opportunities for spiritual reflection, exploration, and growth, such as Bible study, prayer groups, and other fellowship for students and faculty (generally separately). These are voluntary chances for students to gather in community, talk about their faith journeys, and pray for each other's needs, more akin to "youth group" than religion class. By fostering an atmosphere of curiosity, respect, and dialogue, these gatherings allow students and faculty to explore their beliefs, values, and convictions, cultivating a culture of intellectual and spiritual inquiry within the school community.

Chaplains also frequently serve as celebrants for baptisms of students, weddings of alumni, and even occasional funerals for staff members and student family members. At my school, we also recently began our first foray into confirmation preparation. In the past, Episcopal bishops have discouraged school confirmations and baptisms as potentially stepping on the toes of parishes. But recognizing the current reality that the majority of our students have no parish connection, our bishop now allows confirmation classes. Recently, in advance of a diocesan visit to our school, fifteen students and two faculty members signed up to be part of confirmation classes.

Pastoral Care

Most school chaplains consider offering pastoral care and support for the emotional and spiritual wellbeing of students, staff, and families, regardless of religious affiliation, to be a primary role. Through open and nonjudgmental listening, chaplains create safe spaces for students and faculty to explore their joys, fears, and struggles. Whether someone is coping with a personal crisis, grappling with existential questions, or navigating the complexities of friendships, family, or adolescence, the chaplain aims to give compassionate support and guidance, helping students, staff, and families find strength, resilience, and hope in the midst of life's challenges.

Through our presence and intentionality, chaplains can also foster a general sense of belonging and welcome among students and staff. A frequent clergy joke is that preachers really only have one sermon at their core that they give in lots of ways. I think my sermon is that each of us is a beloved child of God, and I am convinced that it is one that most students (and maybe most people) need to hear. In the school setting, this message almost feels prophetic, as we remind the entire school community over and over that God's love is greater than the measures of success that school settings tend to promote (grades, athletic prowess, popularity, etc.).

The importance of the pastoral element of the job is why chaplains need to spend so much time cultivating relationships within the community. Through these relationships, we learn more about the members of our community so that we can truly see and appreciate them for who they are as individuals, and also slowly earn their trust and confidence. While there are some easy ways to signal approachability (like having a candy bowl and comfortable chairs in your office), the main factors in building these relationships are time and presence. This is slow and steady work. Showing up as part of the community is the bulk of the job, whether visiting student groups to show support (especially for marginalized and identity-based affinity groups), cheering on sports events, attending performances, or eating in the faculty room. Chaplains often speak about "creative loitering"—making time to hang out in common spaces so that they are available for the kinds of unstructured and casual interactions that might open opportunities for further connection. Sometimes a stray comment or question can lead to a deeper discussion that helps a student or faculty member to recognize the chaplain as a resource in a time of need.

Part of the job is also modeling faith and prayer in public. For many of our community members, chaplains are stand-ins for religiosity and spirituality that students and faculty may not see in other areas of their lives. Thus we have an opportunity to normalize and personalize both. I don't hesitate to share my stories of frailty, imperfection, and uncertainty—and my own need for forgiveness, love, and growth. And I am open about my experiences of God—a God who is present at all times and in all places loving me just as I am . . . and loving them just as they are.

Shortly after I began offering short meditations at our faculty meetings, several teachers began seeking me out for personal and spiritual counseling. And sometimes student curiosity about my clergy collar or a sermon in chapel can be an entry to a discussion about friendship struggles or questions about faith. Because many of our community members aren't familiar, or maybe comfortable, with religious communities and religious leaders, exposure to our role over time is part of trust building.

In emergencies and tragedies, chaplains also help the school respond with comfort and assistance to those affected. Whether it is the loss of a community member or a tragic world event, chaplains can create supportive spaces for sharing grief and healing, often in conjunction with school counselors. The job of a chaplain is therefore strengthened by being privy to information about the community members' struggles. Early on, the chaplain should try to build trust with administrators and counselors so that they include them whenever possible in information about struggles that students and faculty are facing, enabling chaplains to check in and offer support. Chaplains also collaborate with other school leaders to ensure comprehensive care and address issues that might underlie behavioral concerns.

However, chaplains coming from parish roles may be surprised by the experience of disinterest or hostility towards pastoral care from some families. Whereas our first response to suffering of a parishioner is to check in early and often to offer support and prayer, I have had many experiences of parents asking the adults in the school not to talk to their kids about family tragedies, explaining that the school is their child's "safe space" where they don't have to think about whatever hard thing is going on at home.

Opportunities

1. There are endless and varied opportunities to build relationships outside of worship and classes, from eating lunch in the faculty room, to bringing snacks to a theater rehearsal, to cheering on a basketball game.
2. The parts of school that cause the most anxiety for students present some of the best chances to build relationships and remind them of God's love. One of my favorite ways to be present during exam time is to offer "pre-exam blessings" and healthy snacks to nervous students.

Challenges

1. Sometimes school counselors or administrators might resist including, or not think to include, the chaplain in information or events that enable pastoral care.
2. Time! There is always more to be done and so many pieces of the job vying for the chaplain's attention. And because the student body is cyclical, the work of creating relationships is always in progress.

BRIDGE-BUILDING

And then there is everything else a chaplain does—the "other duties as assigned" of clergy work. This section is admittedly a bit of a catchall for the many other pieces of a chaplain's job that can vary widely from school to school.

Part of a chaplain's ministry is to build bridges among individuals and groups throughout the school and beyond its walls, breaking down what tend to be silos of responsibility in schools. That comes in many forms, from ecumenical and interfaith dialogue and openness, to a commitment to diversity and full inclusion, to working with our local and global communities, to connecting our mission and religious values with our school's practices.

Ecumenical and Interfaith Bridge-Building

In a parish setting, most people in the pews have either signed on to the religious message or at least are actively exploring and open to it. But within a school, we serve a diverse membership, many of whom would never set foot within a church. At my school, because we are part of the Episcopal Church, which tends to be comfortable with religious diversity, we welcome all faiths and require no statement of belief or agreement to doctrine for our students or faculty. As a result, only 20 percent of our students are self-described Episcopalians (and only a portion of them are active churchgoers). Fully a quarter of our students are nonreligious, and almost 10 percent of our families practice a religion other than Christianity.

Of course, a school chaplain's ministry is not only to those that subscribe to the faith we represent. We are also called to walk alongside those of no faith and those of completely different faiths, welcoming and affirming their journeys with sensitivity and respect. Episcopal school chaplains often say that their job is not to create more Episcopalians, or even more Christians, but to encourage everyone in their exploration of and deepening of faith, whatever that might mean for them. Through our openness, we can help to nurture an inclusive culture of respect and understanding between people of different faith traditions and cultural backgrounds, so that all members of the school community are welcomed and valued. In classes, that means inviting different voices and experiences without judgment or tokenization so that all students feel comfortable sharing their own traditions, beliefs, and questions. In chapel, it means more intentional explanations around religious practices, and considering alternative paths of participation, like offering interfaith blessings along with bread and wine during the Eucharist. And in the school community, it means supporting the diversity of our religious affinity groups, and fostering spaces for both intrafaith and interfaith dialogue and understanding.

This is complicated work, and its edges are often unclear. Which holy dates should be on the school calendar? Which religious occasions should be celebrated and by whom? How do we decide what belongs in chapel and what to explore in a more secular setting? Which voices aren't currently represented that we could seek to add to the conversation?

Diversity and Inclusion Bridge-Building

Schools are often intentionally diverse communities, and that is, thankfully, true for my school, where we enroll 28 percent students of color, employ 22 percent faculty of color, and provide financial aid to 22 percent of our students. We have two full-time practitioners that lead us in our work of becoming more inclusive and equitable in our diversity, but as a school we are striving to make our commitment to diversity and inclusion something that belongs to the entire community. We have a long way to go, but the work is definitely underway and included both in our board documents and in our daily practice. Our effort towards diversity, equity, inclusion, and belonging holds a prominent part of the community's education and training; is the focus of student advisory time and faculty professional learning communities; and is an intentional part of curriculum planning and community building.

Although often this work is seen as distinct from the work of the chaplain, in my mind, it is not only closely aligned with the chaplain's work, but clearly stems from the religious identity of the school. If we truly believe that each person is made in the image of God and is a beloved child of God, it is the work of the chaplain to help to create an inclusive and equitable school community that recognizes the innate dignity of every single person so that all of our members develop a sense of true belonging.

The best model for this connection that I've encountered is being done by the Porter-Gaud School in Charleston, South Carolina, where the head chaplain and the head of community engagement and belonging have been incredibly intentional around the connection of their diversity work with their Episcopal identity. See www.portergaud.edu.

Community Bridge-Building

The vast majority of schools in which chaplains work are highly privileged communities. Even if our endowment and funding allows for generous financial aid, because of their high tuition rates, our school communities are generally not representative of the greater communities in which we are located. And so part of the chaplain's job is to help forge connections between our schools and the broader community, living into our call to love others as God has loved us through relationships and service that build compassion and empathy for others.

Many religious schools have a requirement that students fulfill a certain number of "service hours" volunteering in the greater community. However, the purpose of the students' engagement, whether with religious organizations or community groups, local or abroad, hopefully isn't just to collect hours, but to form relationships and engage in service alongside others in the communities in which they serve. Ideally, students will deepen their understanding of the needs of the communities with which they spend time, and emerge with a greater sense of responsibility and empathy towards others. We hope that the time they spend in service learning will complement the experience they have in school and help them develop as ethical leaders in their community and beyond, seeking justice and peace for all people.

Although it isn't a religious organization, one group that does this work especially thoughtfully, and offers training and resources for schools through their Ethical Leadership Forum, is the Shoulder to Shoulder Network. See www.shouldertoshoulder.com and www.ethicalleadershipforum.org.

Mission and Values Bridge-Building

The connections that chaplains help to shape aren't just among individuals and groups in our schools and communities. Our ministry also entails building bridges between the school's own purported values and our actual life together.

Chaplains are stewards of our schools' religious identity. If we are lucky, we have partnership in that work from our admissions team, our head of school, our division directors, our board, and our faculty. But if not (and, realistically, even if so), it is our job to continually educate the various stakeholders about what it means to be an (insert denomination or religion here) school. For most chaplains, that means doing the real work of not just creating talking points about our religious identity, but also looking for ways that there are already connections between that identity and the school's culture and values, and seeking to deepen and further those connections.

We are stewards of our school's mission statements, which, hopefully, are closely aligned with our religious identity. At my school, our mission includes pursuing "goodness as well as knowledge" and "honor[ing] the unique value of each of our members as a child of God." I consider part of my job as chaplain to be ensuring that these aren't just words that we say, but actually a credo that we live. This, of course, is much more easily said than done. These are big and aspirational words, and working to uphold them in deed takes purpose and intentionality. A lot of the focus of this part of the job comes in the form of a chaplain's relationship with their school's administrative team and constant gentle and not-so-gentle reminders to return to what we profess to value.

Opportunities

1. The uniqueness of the chaplain role positions the chaplain to straddle segments of their school, and to effect change and instill vision on a cellular level.
2. Chaplains will never feel like their work is "done" and that there is nothing else to accomplish; there are no dull days!

Challenges

1. Sometimes the work of upholding the school's religious values and mission against the tide of secularism can be lonely and Sisyphean work. Many people working in a religious school, including the administrative leaders, are not there because of any religious connection and may benefit from extensive education and deep relationship work to understand and appreciate the religious mission of the school.
2. Building relationships with administrative leaders, DEIB practitioners, service-learning coordinators, and attending regular meetings with the various stakeholders in a school are critical to a chaplain's role—and they also take significant time away from building relationships with students and faculty, making the job sometimes feel fragmented and impossible.

CONCLUSION

While no school chaplaincy will be the same, the chaplain's role is sure to involve multiple overlapping roles, including leadership of worship, teaching, spiritual formation and pastoral care, and building bridges in the school community and beyond.

This work includes challenges that clergy are unlikely to experience in the usual parish setting. You will feel off-kilter with clergy colleagues and unable to attend most clergy gatherings, and may also feel a bit removed in your mixed role in your school community. You will have to define your role, defend your relevance, and earn the community's trust again and again. You may feel like a small seed in a large and sometimes strange and un-welcoming field.

But overall, school ministry offers incredible opportunities to the chaplain brave enough to enter into this ministry. Schools are creative, diverse settings that will keep you energized, expand your faith, and surprise you every day. (And, with any luck, you will get most weekends and your summers off to reset and renew!) The potential for growth is endless, and the welcome and hospitality you can offer to an incredibly diverse flock looking for rest and belonging is unique in the traditional religious world.

So keep planting, chaplains! And keep faith that God's dreamed-of kingdom is growing through the tiny mustard seed of school ministry.

BIBLIOGRAPHY

National Association of Episcopal Schools. "Principles of Good Practice for Furthering Episcopal Identity in Episcopal Schools." March 18, 2019. https://www.episcopalschools.org/article/principles-of-good-practice-for-furthering-episcopal-identity-in-episcopal-schools/.

7

Moving Church into the World

Religious Education and Practice in Schools

REVEREND DR. STEFANIE TAYLOR

INTRODUCTION

In the United States of America, the first clause in the Bill of Rights states that "Congress shall make no law respecting an establishment of religion." One of the ways this manifests in the country is that religion cannot be spoken about or talked about in public schools. Additionally, in the United States, Christianity is experiencing significant decline. According to the Pew Research Center, Christianity, the largest religion in the United States, experienced a twentieth-century high of 91 percent of the total population in 1976. This declined to 73.7 percent by 2016 and 64 percent in 2022.[1] Due to the rapid decline of the country's largest religion and the lack of religion in public schools, young people in America have fewer options for consistent religious practice. However, students in religious independent schools still have access to religious practice. The purpose of this paper is to discuss the effect of church decline on young people and to highlight the importance of school chaplaincy.

1. Pew, "Pace."

BACKGROUND: A NATIONAL CRISIS

Dr. Lisa Miller, a psychologist from Columbia University who founded the Spirituality and Education Institute, recently published studies proving that spirituality is scientifically measurable; that it exists and that if the development of our spirituality is neglected, we become vulnerable to depression, anxiety, and addiction, just to name a few.[2] She says that neglecting spiritual development is as devastating for human beings as neglecting cognitive development or physical development.

One of her studies shows that girls who go through puberty without a personal connection to the divine are 50 percent more likely to suffer from depression or anxiety as an adult. Teenagers who have a strong relationship to God are 80 percent less likely to abuse substances than the adolescent with a weak relationship. This study was published in the *Journal of the American Academy of Child and Adolescent Psychiatry*.[3]

Dr. Miller and her team have made a direct correlation between mental health decline and spiritual decline. Of course this is not totally new information. The popular recovery method, Alcoholics Anonymous, has twelve steps to recovery that all involve God and a relationship to a "higher power."[4] However, Miller's work is the first peer-reviewed, scientific study that proves that a relationship to a higher power creates protection in our brains against depression, anxiety, addiction, and self-harm.

This is protection young people need. In an article published in *JAMA Pediatrics* this past March, researchers from the Health Resources and Services Administration found that anxiety and depression among children ages three to seventeen has been on the rise for the last five years. The researchers used data from the National Survey of Children's Health, where they looked at trends in children's health, care utilization, and family circumstances from 2016–20.[5] Essentially, at a time when religion is declining, mental health is also declining.

In light of this data, the decline of religion affects more than just churches. It is affecting the mental health of the nation. As such, the way that the United States interprets and practices the first clause of the Bill of Rights must change. If churches are no longer the hub of religious practice

2. Miller, *Awakened*, 45, 87.
3. Miller, *Awakened*.
4. W., *Alcoholics Anonymous*, 30.
5. Lebrun-Harris et al., "Well-Being," 5.

and knowledge, then we need another hub: a place where young people go regularly and a place that provides structure for the passing down of belief and practice. A place like school or work.

This is why chaplaincy is vital. The decline of the church marks the birth of something new: a paradigm shift in how people connect with and experience God. People still want and need to practice their innate spirituality. Research has shown us that fact. However, as our society becomes less communal and more individualistic, places like churches are becoming less relevant or available to people. Now, our community exists in places where we thrive as individuals: schools, work, athletics, etc. Places where individuals are required to go each day. Those places are now the places where people need to be able to meet God and practice their faith.

Fortunately, school chaplaincy has a long history of providing this support for people and has expertise to offer during this communal paradigm shift. Being a school chaplain is different than youth ministry in that school chaplains are able to give sacraments to those whom God puts in front of them, whether that be their daughter's dance teacher, the stranger on the corner, the nurse in the waiting room, or the young people and their families who meet them at school every day. God wants access to them all, and God wants them to feel like they have access to him as well. For many, creed, conformity, and allegiance get in the way of that access. School chaplains get to highlight the gifts of the church without membership. They get to teach about God from many different lenses, and they get to say prayers over the grave of a person who never set foot in a church; they get to put Christ's body in hands that have not declared allegiance, and they get to whisper Christ's love into the ears of all who want to listen.

School chaplaincy is about that delicate dance that includes both a person's love and devotion to the church and their love and devotion to those whom God talks about in John 10:16 (NRSV): "I have other sheep that do not belong to this fold. I must bring them also, and they will listen to my voice. So there will be one flock, one shepherd."

It's different from youth ministry in that way. Youth ministry tends to be underfunded with unrealistic expectations. The result, for many ministers, is that youth ministry can feel overwhelming, lonely, and hopeless. However, school chaplaincy is not the youth ministry of many mainline Christian churches. Schools are funded and supported. Plus, the students are required to be there, and more often than not, they love to be in chapel. Chapel is built into their day and doesn't compete with sleeping in or baseball tournaments. They get to worship freely at school. In this world of working with young people who are free to worship without allegiance or having to choose between worship or something else competing with their time, it also frees chaplains to answer a call to be a priest of the world. They can have a ministry that does not belong to the church alone. This ministry is supported in several different ways: teaching, worship, pastoral care, and even administration.

TEACHING

School chaplains are generally responsible for teaching religion classes. These classes range from doctrinal classes meant to deepen a particular faith to academic classes meant to educate students about all religions or a religion from multiple lenses. Either way, space is given to young people to learn about how a particular faith was founded, lived, and works in the world today. They can read ancient wisdom from scriptures, reflect on their own religious habits or practices, and most importantly, ask questions to an adult with wisdom and experience.

Adolescence is a vital time in the life of a human being. The *International Journal of Mental Health Systems* says, "Adolescence is a critical period of cognitive and behavioral human development. According to Erik Erikson's Social-Emotional Development Theory, it is during this stage when an individual urgently needs to search for a proper role model to answer the big question of who he/she is and his/her moral and spiritual aspects. This formation of identity is a major event in the development of personality and is associated with positive life outcomes."[6] Since access to role models who can and will answer the big questions of life is so vital, these religion classes in schools are essential to the wellbeing of our students.

One chaplain in Georgia described a time when a student asked, "If God is so merciful, why hasn't the devil been forgiven yet?" This chaplain was operating from a model of query and not doctrine and responded, "What would it mean to you if God wasn't so merciful?" From there, the class had a big discussion about what mercy is, how it functions in their lives, and whether or not God is trustworthy. Having space for a conversation like that is typical for school chaplains.

6. Okunev, "Erikson's Life."

CHAPEL/SACRAMENTS

School chaplains design and model worship in schools. This is important because religion is a habit and spirituality is a muscle that needs to be exercised. To be a great basketball player, one must attend practice and build a habit of repetition for the basics of the game. The great ball players still do dribbling, passing, and shooting drills. In the same way, for a person's spirituality to be nurtured, it must be used and practiced. Worship is one way that children can consistently practice their spirituality and/or their religion.

Even if a student personally does not belong to the religion being practiced, they take time out of their day on a regular basis to witness others practicing their faith. This modeling behavior is important to their growth as well. If they grow up watching how one person practices and they form a habit of religious practice by attending chapel, they will have a better understanding of how to add in the regular and consistent practice of their faith in their own life.

Modeling and practice are important. Dr. Miller and her team discovered that a "person's degree of spirituality is determined 29 percent by heredity, and 71 percent by environment. Our spirituality is substantially—roughly two-thirds—a factor of how we're raised, the company we keep, the things we do to build the muscle."[7] Chapel builds the spiritual muscle. It is not the only thing that builds the spiritual muscle, but it provides consistency and a regular break in their lives that is totally devoted to their spirituality. Their environment is oriented toward the regular practice of faith.

In the same vein, school chaplains provide sacraments. Sacraments are defined as outward and visible signs of an inward and spiritual grace. In other words, they are rituals that provide the five senses an awareness or a touchpoint of something big happening in a person's life. The outward and visible sign of baptism is water. The inward, invisible grace that is happening is that God is claiming the person and the Holy Spirit is descending upon them. As incarnational beings, having our senses matched with the invisible work of God in our lives is essential in making it real for us.

Of course a person can engage God in other ways than sacraments. And, the provision of sacraments is a gift to those who either don't know how or don't have the time to create ritual and incarnational opportunities for themselves. Students who go to school where sacraments are provided

7. Miller, *Awakened Brain*, 58.

regularly are students who have their incarnational needs met consistently or get to witness one way of meeting those needs regularly.

PASTORAL CARE

In addition to teaching and providing the sacraments of the church, school chaplains provide pastoral care to the students, families, and faculty/staff at the school. This is different from providing counseling. Counseling is provided by people educated in mental health issues who are trained to help others deal with those issues through specific best practices researched and peer-reviewed in the field of psychology. They are licensed and held accountable by their board and the government.

Pastoral care, on the other hand, is about being with people as they work through all of the experiences a human has in life, both good and bad. If we give advice, it is advice given to us through our sacred Scriptures. However, advice is rarely part of pastoral care. Pastoral care is reminding people that they are not alone, that they are part of something bigger than themselves, that they are loved, and that they are worthy. Moreover, there is nothing that has happened to them and nothing that they have done or can do that can ever separate them from that truth. And if they are having a hard time believing that in the moment, the chaplain stays there with them, prays with them, and offers those gentle reminders as they sit with them.

Pastoral care takes on many different forms in various different schools. At one school in Atlanta, they have a group of parents called "Warrior Wings" who cook meals that are then stored in the school fridge for pastoral emergencies. This is one piece of their care plan. When the chaplain learns that someone is in the hospital or has a death in the family, the chaplain will call someone on the driver's list of Warrior Wings and a meal will be delivered. The goal is for that family to feel seen and cared for by the community.

At another school in Atlanta, they have a three-pronged approach to hospitalizations, deaths, and births: (1) the person gets a phone call or visit from the chaplain, (2) the person gets a meal delivered via an Uber Eats gift card, and (3) the person is put on the prayer list. The idea here is that each person receives the same level of care and the community knows what to expect so if they do fall through the cracks, they can reach out and let someone know they didn't receive part or all of the care plan.

In all cases, a chaplain's job is to pay attention to the community and to respond to the highs and lows in a way that lets each person know they have worth and they are not alone. They know they are being held by a community that loves them for the sake of love; they don't have to do anything or conform to anything in order to be seen and cared for. In this day and age, where loneliness is a national crisis, both the gift of pastoral care and the modeling of pastoral care is crucial.

ADMINISTRATION

Most school chaplains are administrators at their school. Some are on the senior administration level along with the head of school and the top administrators at the school. Some might be on a divisional admin team, some might operate as department chairs or be the direct report for religion teachers. No matter how it happens, most chaplains have a leadership role at the school and serve to advise the school on its identity as a Christian school. This is often the role with the least amount of dedicated time given to it, but it is a vital role nonetheless. Chaplains help orient an organization that is used to operating in the education arena toward operating in the arena of wholeness.

Every school says they educate the "whole child" but not every school provides for the spiritual needs of their students. When they say "whole child," they are talking about academics and character education. School chaplains can ground that character education in something over two thousand years old: the church and its teachings. Chaplains can also provide a role model for good character in God. Work that is grounded in something bigger than ourselves is work that takes hold in a young person's heart. Dr. Miller and her team report over and over that understanding that we are part of something bigger than ourselves is crucial to our spiritual health. With a child's education being rooted in something bigger than their individual goals, their spiritual health is being nourished. If a child's education nourishes their physical, cognitive, and spiritual health, that person will go into adulthood whole. Wholeness, in turn, produces resilience, and resiliency produces a nation of people who know how to problem-solve, to corporate, and to contribute.

SCHOOL CHAPLAINCY AND SECULAR SOCIETY

Research has shown us that having a relationship with the divine is vital for human health and wellness. Churches are in decline and school chaplaincy provides a place where the transfer of support for a divine relationship can happen. But, what does it look like to transfer support for the divine relationship? Should the church allow this transfer of support to happen? The questions can be answered in Scripture.

In John chapter 14, Jesus explains that he is not leaving us alone. He will leave but give us the Holy Spirit. He also explains the function of the Holy Spirit, saying, "But the Advocate, the Holy Spirit, whom the Father will send in my name, will teach you everything, and remind you of all that I have said to you" (John 14:16). Essentially, Jesus is letting us know that it will be easy to forget his words or to understand how to apply them and we will require help. He also is telling us that there is still yet more for us to know and that the Holy Spirit will teach us.

John's Gospel is saying that humans have access to divine knowledge. It is given to us at our birth and is ours to access naturally. This corresponds to the findings in Dr. Miller's research. She writes in her book *The Spiritual Child: The New Science on Parenting for Health and Lifelong Thriving* that unlike cognitive development, where we have to build knowledge and ability from birth, we come into the world fully developed spiritually, and unless we use it, we lose it.[8]

Perhaps this could explain why the church is in decline. If it is true that people need a relationship to the divine for full human development and it is true that we atrophy when we don't get it, then perhaps it is true that organized religion has not been as effective at nurturing spiritual development as it hoped.

For Christians, developing children has always been vital. The sacred texts are clear about the importance of children. We are told that unless we come to God as a little child, we will not receive the kingdom. We are told that God invited the children to come to him and then gave them a place of honor. We are told that wisdom is given to the infants and that we are tasked with bringing our children up in the teachings of God and in a community of faith.

The Bible does not say these things to just the parents of the children. In fact, parents are hardly mentioned. God says these things to the

8. Miller, *Spiritual Child*, 15–25.

community. So whether or not a person has children does not matter in terms of responsibility to the children of the world. We are all accountable to the little ones in our midst who learn by watching those who exist in their world.

When we get it wrong, damage can occur and mental health declines. Dr. Miller made a list of the seven most common ways we turn off our children's spiritual development: (1) Ignoring their spiritual awakening, questions, and experiences. (2) Disavowing their spiritual reality. (3) Discouraging spiritual discovery. (4) Quashing questions. (5) Basing affection or discipline on performance-based values that don't align with spiritual values such as unconditional, noncontingent love, acceptance, and loving guidance. (6) Overlooking the need for a spiritually supportive community. (7) Ignoring signs that a community has punitive or other outdated values of conformity that twist spiritual values to serve dogma.[9]

With these guidelines in place, churches can decide to try and reform if they identify any of this in their community and secular spaces can begin to incorporate spiritual support without being about right practice or authority. The main point is that our children need us to help them develop their spirituality for reasons beyond the fact that they are the future of the church. They need it for their personal wellbeing. They need it so they have the inner strength and resilience necessary to combat a world where Black lives don't matter, where climate change is at catastrophic levels, where democracy is being threatened, family units are getting smaller, and the unforeseen devastating effects of social media begin coming to fruition. School chaplains have experience doing this work already and can help churches if that is the path churches want to take. It doesn't have to be either/or, but it's important to name the shift that is happening and to identify who the new experts at the table are at this moment in time.

Another important point to make is this: it's not too late for adults to reclaim their spiritual selves. As Miller has shown, unlike cognitive or physical development, we come into the world with our spirituality fully developed and intact. The issue for us is that it gets neglected, and just like anything else that gets neglected, it atrophies and causes us problems. But it's still there. It can still be worked and made strong.

As Christians, we must remember that we have been given the Holy Spirit with access to divine knowledge, and we can start thinking about what we need. What are some of the places that stifled our spirituality in

9. Miller, *Spiritual Child*, 40.

childhood or adulthood? What hurts need healing? What old, damaging beliefs still linger in the back of our minds or what dogma that doesn't make sense and forces us into cognitive dissonance with our Creator and our culture exists inside of us?

Because it's not a small thing, these hurts and disconnects. They appear in our lives in the forms of illness or inability to be in relationships. Church is not just about worship or even about outreach. It is about development. If there is no development, there is no evolution, and evolution is the mark of our Creator—our Creator who breathes life into us.

When Jesus says in the Gospel of Matthew, "Let the children come to me. Don't stop them" (Matt 19:14) he meant it beyond just sitting in his lap. He meant that they will come into the world fully loaded with spiritual capacity and they will be expressing it in the world. They must be allowed and encouraged to do so. Jesus knows that coming to him over and over will be necessary for healthy human development and fulfillment. He also knows that without an outlet for this relationship, people will suffer.

As people, it is our responsibility to give all children access to this development. In addition to Dr. Miller's seven ways that we stifle spiritual development, here are her seven ways that we can nurture it: (1) Use spiritual language daily. (2) Transparency and voice: let children hear you use spiritual language as the means by which you work through issues. (3) Meet them where they are. (4) Build spiritual practices together. (5) Embrace relationships with animals and all of nature. (6) Care and repair: show children how to bless and forgive. (7) Live an inspired life where the standard of ethics is not the bare minimum, but rather, the highest standard.[10]

This is no longer an issue for churches alone. This is a community issue. This is a governmental issue. Dr. Miller writes in her book *The Awakened Brain: The New Science of Spirituality and Our Quest for an Inspired Life*, "Our spirituality is substantially—roughly two-thirds—a factor of how we're raised, the company we keep, the things we do to build the muscle."[11] The way that we build that muscle, the attentiveness with which we develop our young people, must be equivalent to how we develop their cognition and their physicality.

As the Gospel reminds us of what has been given to us, let us listen to what the children in our world are saying with the huge rise in mental health issues over the last five years. We must encourage them with spiritual

10. Miller, *Spiritual Child*, 56.

11. Miller, *Awakened Brain*, 48.

language and attention, and in doing so, ignite our own knowing, our own connection, and our own ability to sense the field of love that is thick with divine possibility at all times. As it says in Scripture: "I have created you. . . . I have formed you. . . . Do not fear, for I have redeemed you; I have called you by name, you are mine" (Isa 43:1). We do not need to fear losing the church and we cannot lose God. The God of evolution is calling us into a new paradigm, one where the church goes to the people and loosens its grip on the reigns—a way of being in relationship with God that listens, encourages, and is present daily.

Barbara Brown Taylor, an Episcopal priest and author wrote in her book *Leaving Church: A Memoir of Faith*:

> In a quip that makes the rounds, Jesus preached the coming of the kingdom, but it was the church that came. All these years later, the way many of us are doing church is broken and we know it, even if we do not know what to do about it. We proclaim the priesthood of all believers while we continue with hierarchical clergy, liturgy, and architecture. We follow a Lord who challenged the religious and political institutions of his time while we fund and defend our own. We speak and sing of divine transformation while we do everything in our power to maintain our equilibrium. If redeeming things continue to happen to us in spite of these deep contradictions in our life together, then I think that is because God is faithful even when we are not.[12]

Perhaps now, as churches continue to struggle, we have a real opportunity for growth. Perhaps it is time to step into the next evolution of our relationship to God and each other and to place our spiritual needs not in a compartment, but embedded in our daily lives, in school and in work.

CONCLUSION

Access to regular worship and knowledgeable clergy on a consistent basis will be essential to the health of the people if churches continue to decline.

According to the Reverend Dwight Zscheile, an Episcopal priest and professor, "The overall picture is dire, not one of decline as much as demise within the next generation unless trends change significantly."[13] Due to the work of Dr. Miller's Spirituality and Education Institute, we know that the

12. Taylor, *Leaving Church*, 56.
13. Showalter, "Decline."

demise of the church, if support for a divine relationship is not transferred elsewhere, will be devastating for the mental health of the nation.

Schools are one place this transfer of support for a divine relationship can happen. Research shows that adolescents in religious schools have greater protection against mental health issues than those not in religious schools. According to one article in the *International Journal of Mental Health Systems*, "Religious beliefs also affect how individuals deal with stressful situations, suffering, and life problems as it enhances acceptance and one's ability to function competently in the face of stress and adversity. Religious education reinforces religious coping, which is the use of cognitive behavioral techniques to manage stressful situations in light of one's spirituality or religious beliefs."[14] Essentially, religious schools are one of the few places left in American society that provide regular access to religion and spirituality for young people.

This access is essential to the growth and development of them as people. It aids them in developing a sense of stability in their emerging identity that can withstand life's persistent and common hardships. School chaplains function in schools as the directors of this access. Chaplains design and offer worship, provide pastoral care, teach, and mentor. In this time in human history, chaplains are needed more than ever. Episcopal priest and scholar The Revered Dr. Cynthia Bourgeault once said, "When everything is doing badly and all hope is lost, that is when the great lovers of the world will step up." School chaplains have the great privilege of being part of those great lovers who are tasked with stepping into this paradigm shift in human history.

A NOTE FROM THE AUTHOR

I have a sister and her name is Page. She has wild curly hair, a big smile, and an even bigger personality. I've been told that whenever there are two sisters, one is always the watcher and one is always the dancer. She is definitely the dancer and it's why I hate the Gospel passage about Mary and Martha. I'm clearly Martha, even though I'd love to be Page, er, I mean Mary.

Martha follows the rules and she doesn't stray from the rules even when God himself is standing in her living room. The rules have made her safe. She does not have to worry about what to do when Jesus is standing before her because it's been laid out for her: clean the dishes, put out bread,

14. Estrada et al., "Religious."

fill the glasses, etc. She doesn't have to worry that he won't like her, because she is following the rules. She has chosen safety over something unknown but truly spectacular. Her instinct is to please the Lord rather than to get to know the Lord.

I, too, am a rule follower. I have learned that this is my Achilles' heel. This is what, if I let it, will keep me from knowing God. Because sometimes, I can be right in the middle of celebrating the Eucharist and the body of Christ will be in my hand and the only thing that is on my mind is whether or not I've missed that last note and the choir is going to be upset with me. And then other times, I've been beaten down and scared or hopeless and so I didn't have it in me to follow the rules and the nearness of God was so palpable that all I could do was weep in his presence. Those are the moments that have been etched into my soul and cause me to seek hungrily.

But it's a battle for me. I need structure, I need ritual, and I need to know something, not everything, but something so that I can orient myself in the direction of God and know that it's not just all in my head but is, in fact, real. I need to know that God's name is Jesus. I need to know that he died on the cross for my salvation, and I need to know that he wanted me to love everybody. Those are the bits of information that give God shape and provide a story that tells me who I am.

If you were to tell me, after forty years, that I'm actually adopted and the family history that I grew up knowing wasn't the whole story, I would feel completely lost. In the same way, if you told me that God was more than Jesus and that the story of his life, death, and resurrection wasn't the whole story, I would feel totally lost. But the truth is that I am more than my family history and there is still more for me to discover about myself. This was news to me when I was twenty-five but I'm starting to let that be OK. In the same way, God is more than the story that is told in the Bible and there is still more for us to discover.

The question is: are we Martha or are we Mary? Are we going to miss God when he's standing right in front of us because we are distracted by our tasks: saying our prayers, reciting the Nicene creed, singing a hymn, going to Sunday School . . . or are we going to sit at the Lord's feet and listen to what he has to say? This paradigm shift that I describe in this paper is one that I do not speak about cavalierly. It is one I have struggled with and fought tooth and nail to beat back. I am speaking about it knowing that when I first encountered it, it destroyed my heart and my soul.

But, if I didn't become a priest, I would have been a scientist. Actually, what I want to say is that I did become a scientist when I became a priest. The two go hand in hand for me. My favorite book in seminary was Clayton and Peacocke's *In Whom We Live and Move and Have Our Being: Panentheistic Reflections on God's Presence in a Scientific World*. The book begins with a great line: "The conviction that God is, in principle and by definition, ineffable, beyond all explicit description, greater than we can ever conceive, has in practice not inhibited human beings over the centuries from speculation—and often dogmatic assertion—concerning that same God's relation to the world."[15] In other words, the fact that we all know God is too great to understand has not stopped us from trying to explain him and therefore confine him to fit in a manageable-sized box.

I think in our yearning for God, in our desperation to feel his love and be touched by our Creator again, we hold on tight to what we have learned of him and we never let go, not even to see more of him. We are afraid that when we risk learning more, we will lose him altogether.

And that's a real fear. I'll never forget leaving my evangelical, nondenominational church. I was grasping at anything to get oriented to God again. It was scary. It seemed like there was too much out there and that I would never know the true God. Being in the image of God, it was very easy to cast myself as God. There was nothing to show me the way outside myself and I began to long for that balance sheet my former pastor had shown me. The one where he listed all my sins on one side and all my gifts on the other and then put a line through the debts side with the word "Jesus" scribbled on top. "That's everything," he had said, and I desperately wanted that assurance of certainty again. But you know, it wasn't enough, and my faith began to fall flat. So I had to move forward. I had to move on.

Learning about who God actually is, who we are in relation to that God, and what we are supposed to be doing with this gift of a life is complicated, and we were never meant to figure it out, full stop, and cease to grow. The answers, like us, evolve. And the more we evolve, the more connected we get to God and each other.

But, as a school chaplain, I can tell you that there is a restlessness among young people. I'm beginning to feel like the story isn't enough anymore. I think that restlessness is part of the decline in church membership across the country. People are starting to say things like "The church is dying." Our own bishop is telling new priests that they need to be "bivocational"

15. Clayton and Peacocke, *In Whom We Live*, xviii.

because jobs are drying up and money is disappearing. Church, as we know it, is beginning to shift. And I think the Gospel story about Mary and her sister Martha is telling us that not only is this OK but is good and natural. Martha, Martha . . . there is need of only one thing: to sit and listen.

I believe we are currently in the throes of an evolutionary step forward: we are evolving spiritually. Theologian Matthew Flemming says that "the content and structure of Colossians . . . assert that the universe was ordered by the benevolence of God, who creates through a divine intermediary such as Wisdom or the law. Since humanity was also created in this manner, people possess within themselves the capacity to sense and locate the 'divine order.'"[16]

That text explains to us that we naturally have a private connection to God that pulls us toward him. The kind of connection Dr. Miller and her team have identified is essential in their research. Like the waves of the ocean that are pulled by the moon, so, too, are we gently pulled by God. And I think humanity is beginning to wake up to that pulling on a massive scale. But I'm not sure we allow that private faith to get nurtured by our church because it doesn't always align with the old story or it doesn't seem like there is a place for it.

To give you an example of what I mean, I know that there are people in the Episcopal Church who don't believe that it matters that Jesus died on the cross. I also know that there are people in the church who believe that Jesus dying on the cross is the only thing that matters.

Yet, we don't talk about it. I have my faith and you have yours and we come together to share in Christ's body and blood once a week and we call it a day. But the church cannot evolve along with us if we don't share our truths with each other.

In Mary and Martha's story, Jesus is telling us that he is standing right in front of us and he doesn't want us to miss him. He is giving us permission to let go a little bit and he is telling us that we are not going to lose him when we do. The fact that Mary is not doing what she is supposed to be doing and is instead simply listening has been noticed by Jesus and he says, "Mary has chosen the better part, which will not be taken away from her" (see Luke 10:38–42 NRSVue). So as we go through this paradigm shift in religion, as we let chaplaincy take up more space in the world, let us be present to this moment. Let's be open to what is coming up for us and how

16. Miller, *Awakened Brain*, 4.

we are asked to move forward. And let's be a community that nurtures one another's truth.

BIBLIOGRAPHY

Clayton, Philip, and Arthur Peacocke. *In Whom We Live and Move and Have Our Being: Panentheistic Reflections on God's Presence in a Scientific World.* Grand Rapids: Eerdmans, 2004.

Estrada, Crystal Amiel, et al. "Religious Education Can Contribute to Adolescent Mental Health in School Settings." *International Journal of Mental Health Systems* 13 (2019). https://pubmed.ncbi.nlm.nih.gov/31057663/.

Lebrun-Harris, Lydie A., et al. "Five-Year Trends in U.S. Children's Health and Well-Being, 2016–2020." *JAMA Pediatr.* (2022). https://jamanetwork.com/journals/jamapediatrics/fullarticle/2789946.

Masters, Kim J., et al. "Practice Parameter for the Prevention and Management of Aggressive Behavior in Child and Adolescent Psychiatric Institutions, with Special Reference to Seclusion and Restraint." *Journal of the American Academy of Child & Adolescent Psychiatry* 41 (2002) 206–14.

Miller, Lisa. *The Awakened Brain: The New Science of Spirituality and Our Quest for an Inspired Life.* 1st ed. New York: Random House, 2021.

———. *The Spiritual Child: The New Science on Parenting for Health and Lifelong Thriving.* 2nd ed. New York: Picador, 2016.

Okunev, Rhoda. "Erikson's Life and Psychosocial Developmental Stages." *The Psychology of Evolving Technology* (2022) 49–56.

Pew Research Center. "In U.S., Decline of Christianity Continues at Rapid Pace." October 17, 2019. https://www.pewresearch.org/religion/2019/10/17/in-u-s-decline-of-christianity-continues-at-rapid-pace/.

Showalter, Brandon. "Episcopal Church Will Be Dead in 20 Years, Researcher Says; Denomination Continues 'Dire' Decline." The Aquila Report, December 7, 2020. https://theaquilareport.com/episcopal-church-will-be-dead-in-20-years-researcher-says-denomination-continues-dire-decline/.

Taylor, Barbara Brown. *Leaving Church: A Memoir of Faith.* 1st ed. New York: HarperOne, 2012.

W., Bill. *Alcoholics Anonymous: The Big Book.* 1st ed. New York: Alcoholics Anonymous World Services, 2002.

8

British Military Chaplaincy

GILES LEGOOD

INTRODUCTION

Today's military chaplains stand in a long line of clergy who have worked outside a parochial or congregational setting. Throughout most of the history of the church, there have been clergy who have ministered alongside people in their times of vulnerability and in their times of strength, in settings that have not been primarily church-based. Over the past two centuries, clergy have worked in hospitals, schools, prisons, and, in the twentieth century, in a wider range of sectors and settings. Whilst there was a massive increase in the numbers of clergy serving with the armed forces during the First World War, the concept of clergy ministering in such a setting is no modern phenomenon. For centuries in Britain clergy have served with and alongside fighting forces.

In this chapter, we shall first outline a history of clerical involvement with British fighting forces. In doing so, we shall note the purpose, organization, and differing forms of delivery of ordained ministry to naval, army, and air force personnel. As part of this storytelling, we shall consider notable examples of sacrificial ministry from twentieth-century chaplains of all three Services. The latter part of the paper will move on to look at some of the lessons identified for chaplaincy by chaplains and others who have reflected on the more recent conflicts in Iraq (Operation TELIC), Afghanistan (Operation HERRICK), and the wider Middle East (Operation KIPION). Finally, the paper will identify some of the current challenges and strengths for armed forces' chaplaincy in the twenty-first century as it looks to meet the future religious, pastoral, and ethical needs of military personnel. It will raise questions for discussion and consideration which those from other sectors may find of relevance to their own contexts and may also assist in offering an external critique on the sector under consideration.

A HISTORY OF BRITISH MILITARY CHAPLAINCY

The larger medieval households of England often contained regular garrisons of soldiers and these would require the attention of a designated cleric to act as chaplain. The concept of a single, homogenous "British" army is a relatively modern one. Chaplains were employed by individual, freestanding regiments until 1796 when a Royal Warrant was issued, bringing the Army Chaplains' Department into being. Although a decree was passed by the Synod of Westminster in 1175 that no cleric should take up arms or go about in armor, there was no war fought or army raised in England before 1350 which did not have a leading member of the clergy as one of its commanders. As early as 447, Germanus, bishop of Auxerre, visited Britain and led troops in Wales to a victory over the Saxons and Picts, teaching them, it is said, the war cry "Alleluia." Bede tells us that clergy had leading parts to play in other battles in Wales, Chester, York, Scotland, and elsewhere.

By the time of the reign of Edward I, however (1272–1307), the age of combative clergy was virtually at an end. Instead, priests accompanied kings and knights into battle, including for instance at the Battle of Crecy (1346) where on the eve of battle King Edward III of England retired to his oratory to pray and the next morning rose early to hear Mass and receive communion whilst his army made their confessions and prepared for battle. At the battle three types of clergy are recorded: those acting as the king's confessors and ecclesiastical secretaries; those serving under a baron or other nobleman; and those serving the Welshmen (recorded as those most poorly paid). It is significant to note that these clergy were accompanying the army wherever it went to battle. The chaplains were not remaining on English soil but were traveling to minister wherever their charges went. Thomas Eltham, a chaplain who went to Agincourt in 1414, mentions two classes of chaplains: those thirty-two belonging to the king's retinue and another class attached to the nobles. It was not until the late sixteenth and early seventeenth centuries, however, that regiments as we might recognize them came to be formed. As they were formed, terms like "colonel" and "sergeant major" first came to be used and, significantly for us, the terms "preacher" and "chaplain" also begin to appear on the payrolls. The command headquarters of the first national regular army, Cromwell's New Model Army of the 1640s, lists a "Master Bowles—Chaplain to the Army." During the Puritan Revolution, it was not only the Puritans who had their own (Puritan) chaplains but the Royalist forces too. The Royalists appointed their own Anglican clergy as chaplains. At the same time, those Scottish forces of the Solemn League and Covenant loyal to the king, Charles II, were ministered to by Presbyterian chaplains representing Scotland's established religion. It was Charles II who became the first monarch to maintain a standing army in peacetime. Although the task of appointing a chaplain to a regiment fell to the colonels commanding, such provision was often little more than that of a religious functionary. Like their civilian counterparts, chaplains could absent themselves from their duties and employ a more poorly paid clergyman to carry out their duties for them. One chaplain noted that "the Chaplaincy is generally a kind of sinecure and the care of souls is left to any worthless wretch that will do it at an easy rate." When we lay in one city, the care of four or five regiments was left to an unhappy man, who was an object of common ridicule among the soldiers for his perpetual drunkenness. Such piecemeal and insufficient ministry was abolished in September 1796 when Royal Warrant founded the Army Chaplains' Department.

The experience of fighting the French in North America and expatriates in the War of American Independence had underlined the impressions amongst those responsible for the army's morale that a larger, more permanent, and better-equipped chaplaincy was required. On taking office the first chaplain-general, the Reverend John Gamble, found that 340 regimental chaplains were on leave and so required them to return to their duties by the end of the year or be pensioned off. Almost all of the chaplains within the new Department were members of the Church of England, although a few were Presbyterians. By 1827 the numbers of Presbyterian chaplains had grown to such an extent that they became a separate branch of the Department. In 1794, Father Alexander MacDonnell became the first Roman Catholic chaplain to serve in the British Army since the reign of James II (1685–88). Following the Catholic Emancipation Bill of 1829, Roman Catholic chaplains were regularized within the army in 1836 and Catholic troops were permitted to attend Mass in Catholic chapels close to their barracks, provided that their commanding officer approved (mostly these troops served in Irish regiments).

The first known priest to accompany a fleet from Britain was Odo (later Archbishop of Canterbury, who died in 959), who traveled with King Athelstan in the tenth century.[1] Outside Britain, we know that around the year 1000, a priest accompanied the Norse explorer Leif Erikson on a voyage to what we now call North America.[2] The earliest known reference to a priest aboard English fighting ships, however, comes from the time of the Second Crusade of 1147 when an expedition set out (which resulted in the capture of Lisbon) with the following in its orders: "That every ship should have its own priest, and that there should be orders to observe the same practices as in a parish. . . . That everyone should confess weekly and go to communion on the Lord's Day." During the reign of King John (1199–1216), William de Wrotham, archdeacon of Taunton, is recorded as being the first "Keeper of the King's Ships."[3] This was not a chaplaincy role but an example, like in the armies, of fighting clerics being intimately involved in the life of the military. During the pilgrimages to the shrine of St. James at Compostela in Spain and other places in Europe and the Holy Land, begun in the middle of the fifteenth century, priests were aboard the ships carrying the pilgrims. In the latter part of the same century priests sailed on galleon ships during what has been called the Age of Discovery. On these journeys they sought both to establish the church wherever they went and to minister to the sailors and other travelers. In the military context, however, it was not until the sixteenth century that chaplains were employed to accompany the fleet with a role which was other than operational, but rather spiritual. In 1626 King Charles I ordered that chaplains should sail on all ships of his naval fleet and in 1653 public worship was made mandatory on all ships of the English navy. By the period 1689–1713, records show that over seven hundred chaplains were appointed in this time. Names of chaplains show, however, that many appointments consisted of just one voyage and that chaplains also retained their parish benefices whilst serving the navy. This was not the case, however, with the Reverend Alexander Scott, chaplain of HMS *Victory*, in whose arms Admiral Nelson died at the Battle of Trafalgar on October 21, 1805. As with chaplains to the various British regiments, there was a high degree of absenteeism amongst the chaplains

1. Smith, *Military*, 1.
2. Down, *Chaplains*, 11.
3. Gerrard, "Military Activities."

and widespread hiring of younger clergy to perform the chaplain's role on another's behalf.

Unlike in the army, where we are able to say precisely when the Army Chaplains' Department officially came into being, the command structure within the navy emerged more gradually. Indeed, it may be for this reason that there is much less published material, in book form, on the work of naval chaplains. The first person to be given the title "Chaplain-Generall [*sic*] of the Fleet" was William Hodge in 1701. Between 1812 and 1815, John Owen, chaplain-general of the Army, also served as "chaplain-general of the Fleet." In 1859 the senior chaplain at Greenwich Hospital was recognized as "head of the Naval Chaplains" and "chaplain to the Fleet." Since 1902 the title and scope of the authority of the navy's most senior chaplain has been established as "chaplain of the Fleet."

Towards the end of the First World War, on April 1, 1918, the Royal Air Force (RAF) was formed as an amalgamation of the army's Royal Flying Corps and the Royal Naval Air Service. In the first few months of the new Service's life chaplains were borrowed from the navy and army. A Royal Navy chaplain, the Reverend Harry Viener, was seconded to the RAF to create an RAF Chaplaincy Service. Viener became the RAF's first chaplain-in-chief. He created a chaplaincy of sixty chaplains, drawn from the navy, army, and civilian life. When the war ended the RAF, like the navy and army, reduced in size and so too did its chaplaincy. The RAF had just twenty-nine chaplains by 1919, though this increased to thirty-six by 1931. As a Royal Navy chaplain, Viener had originally intended that chaplains should wear uniform without rank (as Royal naval chaplains still do to this day). However, confusion with church army officers and uniformed canteen workers led him to think that this solution was unworkable. As a consequence, he produced a compromise in which chaplains would wear a rank relative to the seniority or appointment within the Service. In effect, this meant that chaplains were expected to wear rank for identification and for a position within the RAF hierarchy but explicitly not to exercise executive powers which might separate the chaplain from noncommissioned ranks.

During the interwar years a pattern of RAF chaplaincy emerged which gave it a character different from the chaplaincies in the other two Services. In the army, as we have seen, chaplains have tended to be attached to regiments, following them wherever they are sent and being alongside them in whatever task they undertake. In the Royal Navy, chaplains have tended to be attached to ships and have sailed with the ship's company wherever it is sent. The Royal

Air Force, in many respects, has been a more static force. RAF personnel operate from and live at RAF Stations which are, of course, immovable. The model of ministry of RAF chaplaincy, therefore, has for large parts of its history been like that of a parochial model where the community lives, works, and socializes in one place. Where RAF personnel have deployed on combat operations, this has meant that some personnel from several stations "go to war," and whilst a chaplain may go with them, it is not necessarily a chaplain who already knows those who are deploying. Whilst Service personnel are away from home, the unit chaplain will still be ministering to those left at home and to the families of those who have deployed.

During the Second World War, the size of the RAF increased to over a million servicemen and women and proportionally the size of the chaplaincy increased (to over one thousand clergy). The vast majority of these clergy joined simply for the duration of war and returned to their civilian ministries thereafter. In a similar vein the chaplaincies of the Naval Chaplaincy Service and the Royal Army Chaplains' Department grew and shrank accordingly.

There is a significant and substantial body of evidence that during both World Wars armed forces' chaplains fulfilled their calling in representing the church in the heart of the military community. Padre Noel Mellish, aged thirty-five, was an army chaplain on March 27, 1916, when an attack on the St. Eloi Crater on the Ypres Salient was launched. Several enormous mines were exploded under the German trenches and the British troops then attacked. They moved forward and were met by intense rifle, machine gun, and artillery fire. The battalion to which Mellish was attached suffered huge losses. Over three days, Mellish repeatedly went out, under machine gun fire, to bring in the wounded. On the first day, without assistance, he rescued ten wounded men, on the second day he brought back a further twelve, and on the third day, with volunteers, he went to rescue the remaining wounded. For this he was awarded the highest award for gallantry, the Victoria Cross.

Padre Geoffrey Harding was an RAF chaplain, attached to a mobile radio unit, who was on the beaches of Normandy on D-Day, June 6, 1944. He won the Military Cross for, in the words of his award's citation, "his gallantry and disregard for his own safety"[4] In the carnage of the military engagement that day (there was a 25 percent casualty rate for those who

4. *London Gazette*, "Military Cross" (London, UK), November 10, 1944, cited in Traces of War, "Harding, Geoffrey Clarence."

landed on the beach), Harding walked to the neighboring village, to a house where a number of snipers were located, and secured some water for those on the beach. He spent all day ministering to those who were wounded or dying. Years later when being interviewed about this engagement, which the military named Operation OVERLORD, Harding remarked, "Someone told me at the time I walked up and down the beach calmly as if I were walking up and down the aisle in the church, but that was simply due to the fact that I am constitutionally lazy and refused to be hurried, least of all by the enemy."[5]

The Reverend Christopher "Kit" Tanner, a Royal Navy chaplain, was aboard HMS *Fiji* in 1941 when it was bombed by German Junkers and Stuka aircraft—370 bombs were aimed at *Fiji* during the day. When the order came to "abandon ship," Kit Tanner moved to the sick bay where there were sixty wounded men. Tanner personally supervised their removal to another ship, the one whaler which was left in service. "He was untiring in his ministrations," said his Captain, "and forgot nobody."[6] When the time came for him to jump into the sea he found that he had a new parish, approximately half a square mile of choppy Mediterranean. When the men in the sea saw the two remaining British destroyers withdraw from the scene some of them lost heart and drowned. In the water, Kit Tanner was a constant tower of strength. He helped men too far gone to help themselves to the floats. He administered the life-saver's shock treatment—a well-aimed right hook to the jaw—to a young seaman in the grip of terrible panic. He assisted a sailor with his arm blown off, who subsequently survived. He led men in singing and the strains of "Roll out the Barrel" could be heard in the night. There were other songs, many of which he had heard sung in the bar of the Gloucester Rugby Football Club.

Shortly after midnight, cheering started and torches were flashed as it became clear that HMS *Kandahar* and HMS *Kingston* had come for them. Aboard HMS *Kandahar*, there were blankets, hot drinks, and cigarettes for *Fiji*'s survivors. Kit Tanner was brought aboard HMS *Kandahar* but did not relax from his duties. There were still men in the sea who were too far gone through exhaustion to grasp the ropes lowered to them from the destroyer. Tanner made these men his special responsibility. Thirty-four officers and

5. *London Gazette*, "Military Cross" (London, UK), November 10, 1944, cited in Traces of War, "Harding, Geoffrey Clarence."

6. *London Gazette*, "Military Cross" (London, UK), November 10, 1944, cited in Traces of War, "Harding, Geoffrey Clarence."

500 men were saved out of *Fiji*'s total complement of 700. Nearly 30 of these men owed their lives to Tanner. No accurate count was possible of the number of times he dived from HMS *Kandahar* to bring in yet another man. Finally, only one man remained to be brought aboard. Despite his exhaustion Padre Tanner made a last effort to save him and brought him safely on board. When hauled up himself the padre died within a few minutes of exhaustion. For these acts of bravery Tanner was posthumously awarded the Albert Medal.

For generations chaplains have played their part and served with great distinction, devotion, and courage alongside sailors, soldiers, and air force personnel. Modern-day chaplains in the armed forces have responded to a call from God, with the permission of their sending church, to exercise their ministry in the military. To do so they need to be part of a "profession within a profession." The Chaplain in Chief US Army in August 2011 wrote: "We are professional pastors, and we have a total ministry to the entire community. Perhaps more than anyone else, we can provide the leadership, personal openness and acceptance, and professional expertise which commanders need in order to have a positive and healthy environment, a climate of moral responsibility, and community of openness and trust."[7]

In his book *Creative Ministry*, the priest Henri Nouwen addresses the concern between professionalism and spirituality within ministry. Nouwen wrote: "If a minister wants to be of real help in his contact with people, he has to be a professional with special information, special training, and special skills. But if he wants to break through the chains of our manipulative world, he has to move beyond professionalism, and through self-denial and contemplation, become a faithful witness of God's covenant."[8] In a continuum of service and sacrifice, chaplains in the military have demonstrated in peace and in war that they do have a special place and can be professional in the most hostile of environments. They have done so by self-denial and self-sacrifice and been recognized in the services for their faithful witness to the military community.

7. Gerhardt W. Hyatt, as quoted in Councell, "Resourcing," 9.

8. Nouwen, *Ministry*, 12.

LESSONS IDENTIFIED—INSIGHTS AND REFLECTIONS OF CHAPLAINS DEPLOYED ON OPERATIONS TELIC AND HERRICK: THREE PERSPECTIVES

The Royal Navy

Deployed naval chaplains often work in singleton jobs with no support from like-minded team members, and as a result are always "on the job" whilst deployed. It is crucial that appropriate self-care is maintained to help prevent burnout, allowing for reflection and an oasis for the spirit. Recent comments from Operation KIPION suggest that there are many in the Royal Navy who do not understand the wider contribution a chaplain can make to the life of a ship or unit, beyond worship services, prayers, and reactive pastoral care, and need to be educated in the proactive and preventative pastoral work a chaplain can undertake to enhance the holistic care of people.

Ideally a period of shore time will be achievable before the chaplain's next deployment. This should be used to offer pastoral care to the ship's company or unit as they adjust to being back in the United Kingdom, whilst allowing the chaplain to unlatch from the ship's company or unit and tie up any loose pastoral ends before deploying again. Deploying in a singleton role carries with it a myriad of emotions and presents many challenges on both a spiritual and personal level. A cultural climate where support and advice is both offered and asked for without hesitation or embarrassment, given and received with grace and compassion, is essential for the development and fulfillment of the chaplain in their role and avoidance of a sense that chaplains are of high value but low priority.

The Army Perspective

From an army perspective a chaplain will usually deploy as part of a team—which may have Tri-Service elements—for a period of six months. With pre-deployment training and post-tour leave the operational cycle usually involves a twelve-month period. Reserve chaplains usually deploy to a specific unit—such as a medical field hospital—and only occasionally will deploy with their own soldiers. Team cohesion is a key strength and helps to overcome fear and isolation.

> During deployment the need for spiritual resilience was considered to be a key to successful and enduring ministry and the importance of partnering/mentoring/shepherding of each other is vital. . . . The Post Op Retreat is key to the "closure" of the Team experience . . . and should be conducted in a safe space suitable for decompression and normalisation—especially in terms of renewing the Priestly vocation and life after a long term on Ops. This post-tour support is one factor that gives Chaplains confidence for future Ops and builds spiritual resilience.[9]

The Royal Air Force Perspective

"Timely preparation for deployment is essential and the key to reducing anxiety and allowing a successful deployment."[10] During deployment it is often recognized that some chaplains would have appreciated someone being identified as a point for open and honest dialogue (within confidentiality guidelines). From a spiritual perspective it is also felt important to identify at an early stage corporate prayer times with other chaplains, other Christians, or both. There is also a need for each chaplain to remember why we are there and ultimately who has called us there.

Undoubtedly each chaplain's spiritual robustness is the key to a good and productive deployment. It should be seen as paramount for each chaplain to keep their faith nurtured and healthy prior to, during and after each deployment. Rabbi Stephen Roberts and Reverend William Ashley Sr., in their book *Disaster Spiritual Care*, write that: "It is often the simple presence of a person of God that provides healing and comfort. The ministry of solidarity and accompaniment, of silence in the face of tragedy, of surrender to the God of our understanding, is often the most we can do in such situations."[11] During the conflict in Afghanistan (Operation HERRICK, 2001–14) chaplains of all three Services were deployed to be the chaplain attached to the UK Medical Group, most specifically to the hospital at Camp Bastion. Many of the chaplains who carried out this work regard it as one of the most profound times of their ministry. They were moved and changed by what they experienced, for good or for ill. One RAF chaplain, the Reverend Nick Barry, when reflecting on his time at the hospital, talked about

9. United Kingdom, AFCPB, "Policy Documents."
10. United Kingdom, AFCPB, "Policy Documents."
11. Roberts and Ashley Sr., *Disaster*, 15.

the ministry of prayer, presence, and proclamation in saying the Prayer of Commendation at the point of death in the hospital's emergency department. Echoing the words of the RAF Chaplains' Branch motto, *ministrare non ministrari* (to serve, not to be served), Padre Barry recalls the simple but powerful words said to him in conversation with a military nurse.

This conversation took place in a setting not so dissimilar from a scene from the television program *MASH*, with the life-saving medical equipment and blood-stained evidence of the fragility of human life all around. Padre Barry noted that he became aware of a "significant evangelistic component to the words of commendation which are not so easily apparent at, for instance, the sterile, gentle bedside in a nursing home in the UK where death might not be unexpected. Standing on the blood-soaked floor in Bastion hospital [*sic*] there was no clear teaching or preaching, just the liturgical moment where ministry offered a glimpse away from the present location, a glimpse of redemption." In all three Services, the loss of a colleague is felt deeply, especially when that person is killed in action: "In these situations, many soldiers come to the chaplain to speak about how they are feeling. Some speak about regrets, their questions, their fears and their guilt. Others come because they are experiencing grief for the first time and they are not sure whether their emotions and physical sensations are normal. Such conversations are not necessarily religious, but are born out of the Church's desire to care for the soldier's most human needs. Sometimes prayer is appropriate, sometimes not. Some soldiers want to talk about heaven, others suspect there is nothing but darkness. Each soldier, religious or not, uses the chaplain to process his or her thoughts and adjust to a new reality, which sadly often includes the pain of loss and the process of grief."

The Aftermath

On October 26, 2014, after thirteen years in Afghanistan and eight years of bloody fighting in Helmand that cost the lives of 453 British servicemen and women, Camp Bastion, which was once the largest British military base in the world, was finally closed. At its busiest Bastion housed up to 14,000 troops and more than a dozen chaplains. In the height of the fighting there were up to six hundred aircraft sorties per day. According to the BBC News the Afghan War cost more than £20bn. In the years following British and other allies' withdrawal, across the country 6.7 million Afghan children go to school, nearly half of them girls. At the same time healthcare improved and life expectancy is longer. It was thought that the Taliban threat had been substantially curtailed, and yet by 2021 the elected Afghani government fell, the president fled the country, and, once more, the Taliban controlled the nation. In the ten years since the British government brought its troops home, a new focus has emerged for the British Armed Forces. The shift from a long-term war in Afghanistan meant a transition to contingency operations where troops were prepared to react to crisis around the world, be it overflying Syria, patrolling the Strait of Hormuz (which is considered one of the most strategic, if not the most strategic, straits of water on the planet), providing short-term training teams to the Middle East, or delivering real-time healthcare and medical support to Ebola victims in Sierra Leone. The range of challenge and threat endures and chaplains of all three Services need to be ready and willing to serve alongside. Arguably the world is in its most fragile state since the end of the Second World War, nearly eighty years ago. The reemerging bullishness of Russia, the emerging challenge of China, the shifting dynamic of the Middle East, and the lawlessness of much of central Africa may mean that armed forces may be required in various theaters of war simultaneously.

At the closure of Camp Bastion Brigadier Rob Thomson, the most senior British officer in Helmand, said: "I think there are three emotions at play. We are proud of what our service men and women have done. We are happy and sad. We are happy we are all going back to our families but we are also sad because we are leaving behind some friends who were courageous on the battlefield. We have made a difference on the streets of Britain and in Afghanistan. This is not defeat or victory. We have an army that is hugely adaptable and can adjust in step as we enter a new campaign."[12]

The challenge for chaplaincy in all three services is how we are to also step up to the mark and prepare for contingency. Inevitably there will be greater joint-force commitments where chaplains of all Services will serve together. There will also be a great reliance upon reservist chaplains and pressure upon a diminishing pool of clergy. Questions about humanism and world faith religions other than Christianity will prevail and need to be addressed. So too will the demand from each of the single Services for chaplains to serve "cloth on cloth": the Naval Chaplaincy Service with the RN, the Royal Army Chaplains' Department with the Army, and the Royal Air Force Chaplains' Branch with the RAF. More will be asked but more

12. Quoted from a talk given in the Helmand Province of Afghanistan during a ceremony marking the end of UK combat operations in Helmand.

will be given by chaplains who feel called by God to serve alongside those who serve in the Forces of the Crown.

QUESTIONS FOR CONSIDERATION

1. What are the opportunities and challenges presented to military chaplains, given that they have loyalties to both the institutions they serve and those that send them? What are the role tensions felt here?
2. Royal Navy chaplains do not wear rank but, by custom, adopt the rank of the person they are speaking to. Army and Royal Air Force chaplains wear rank and exercise executive authority. What are the benefits and demerits of each?
3. Humanists serve in the public sector as chaplains in both HM's Prison Service and the National Health Service. Soon to be selected, trained, and commissioned in the armed forces, how might some see this as departing too far from received norms of chaplaincy?
4. British military chaplains are noncombatant and do not carry weapons. Chaplains from other nations do bear arms, whilst some others have an armed assistant attached to them. How might each form of chaplaincy expression be perceived?

BIBLIOGRAPHY

Councell, Gary R. "Resourcing the Chaplaincy in the Post-Vietnam Years, 1973 Thru 1993." https://apps.dtic.mil/sti/tr/pdf/ADA280351.pdf.

Down, Kevin. *Chaplains of the Royal Navy*. London: HMSO, 1989.

Gerrard, Daniel M. G. "The Military Activities of Bishops, Abbots and Other Clergy in England c. 900–1200." Medievalists.net. https://www.medievalists.net/2011/10/the-military-activities-of-bishops-abbots-and-other-clergy-in-england-c-900-1200/.

Nouwen, Henri J. M. *Creative Ministry*. New York: Doubleday, 1971.

Roberts, Stephen B., and Willard W. C. Ashley Sr., eds. *Disaster Spiritual Care: Practical Clergy Responses to Community, Regional and National Tragedy*. Woodstock, VT: Skylight Paths, 2006.

Smith, Wilfrid. *A History of Military Chaplaincy*. London: Aldershot, 1961.

Traces of War. "Harding, Geoffrey Clarence." https://www.tracesofwar.com/persons/63880/Harding-Geoffrey-Clarence.htm.

9

Raising Vocations for Military Chaplaincy

ANN RITONIA

Military chaplaincy, like other forms of chaplaincy within the federal government, is a vocation within a vocation. Chaplains are first called to be ministers within a specific religious faith group and then compelled for a variety of reasons, but most importantly a calling from God, to live out the practice of their ministry serving a particular constituency or ministry context. In the Episcopal Church, the perspective from which this is written, raising vocations for military chaplaincy is challenging but also an unparalleled opportunity to live out Jesus's mandate to "go therefore and make disciples of all nations, baptizing them in the name of the Father and of the Son and of the Holy Spirit, and teaching them to obey everything that I have commanded you" (Matt 28:19–20 NRSV).

Military chaplaincy is complex, extremely rewarding, and not for every priest. It is also one of the most challenging and varied forms of ministry outside the institutional church and far away from Episcopal communities that form and raise up ministers of the gospel. Because of this distance from the center of the institutional church, Episcopal priests called to military chaplaincy must first be grounded in Scripture, prayer, theology, doctrine, liturgical practice, and Anglican identity prior to service as a military chaplain. This grounding will provide a foundation upon which to stand and hold on to in times of duress and especially in the fog of war. Military chaplains not only attend to the spiritual needs and moral wellbeing of Episcopalians but to all military members and their families wherever they serve. This ministry of care and presence is an invitation to enter into the lives of military service members at all levels of command and build bonds of trust and compassion that have the potential to transform lives as military members experience their innate value as beloved children of God through the care of their chaplain.

Military chaplains are ordained clergy (or endorsed lay leaders when a denomination does not ordain) from over two hundred Department-of-Defense-recognized denominations or faith groups. Every military chaplain is a commissioned officer in the Armed Forces, and as noncombatants, they ensure that all service members have the right to observe the tenets of their religion, or to observe no religion at all in accordance with the Free Exercise Clause of the First Amendment to the Constitution of the United States. Of importance is that in accordance with Section 533(b) of Public Law 112–239, as implemented by DoD Instruction 1304.28, "no Service member may require a chaplain to perform any rite, ritual, or ceremony that is contrary to the conscience, moral principles, or religious beliefs of the chaplain, nor may any Service member discriminate or take any adverse personnel action on the basis of the refusal by the chaplain to comply with such requirements."[1] This DoD instruction is significant as it especially impacts the spiritual support and care that military members who identify as LGBTQIA+ may or may not receive based on the religious beliefs of military chaplains. With the proliferation of extremely conservative chaplains in the Armed Forces, and the small number of progressive chaplains able to minister to this already vulnerable population, this marginalized group of military members don't always have access to the spiritual and sacramental support they need in order to exercise their religious freedom. The importance of raising up Episcopal military chaplains to provide spiritual care to our LGBTQIA+ siblings cannot be overstated.

Military chaplains lead religious services, provide for religious accommodations for all service members, and perform counseling on a variety of issues to include but not limited to: marriage, grief, finances, sexuality, trauma, abuse, workplace conflict, combat stress, suicide, moral injury, and faith. All chaplains, unlike licensed counselors that serve the military, adhere to 100 percent confidentiality even in matters that might affect mission readiness or the safety of the service member or others. When military members seek the counsel of a chaplain the encounter is sacramental in

1. DoD Instruction 1304.28, Pub. L. No. 112–239, sec. 533(b) (2004).

nature and akin to entering a confessional with the seal to remain unbroken. Time spent with a chaplain is the only place in the military chain of command that is held to this standard of confidentiality. Chaplains also advise commanders on the religious and moral landscape of their commands and locales as well as accompany service members into combat and address combat stress and moral injury. They help service members deal with all manner of life challenges and at their best provide hope and healing. Chaplains work with members of the military at all levels of rank and command, but especially as junior officers, most of their time is spent with eighteen-to-twenty-six-year-old service members, helping them in the process of "adulting." Chaplains observe this is increasingly common as many young adults, especially those who join the military seeking educational and economic opportunity, have experienced significant trauma prior to military service or have not been nurtured well. Given the nature of military service, chaplains and senior noncommissioned officers often find themselves filling the psychological and social support gaps previously satisfied by family, religious organizations, and the local community. For those seeking to live out their baptismal promises, reaching out to the lost and marginalized in a pluralistic environment, and evangelizing the unchurched in creative, incarnational, and life-giving ways, military chaplaincy can provide a very large mission field.

Given the complexity and skills needed for military chaplaincy, the challenges to raising vocations for this unique ministry in the Episcopal Church are many but certainly not insurmountable. Those challenges include:

- A shrinking pool of candidates seeking ordination to the priesthood, as evidenced by declining enrollment at Episcopal seminaries and diocesan formation programs reducing the number of candidates available to even consider military chaplaincy.
- Decreased focus and funding of campus ministry and young adult ministry both nationally and at the diocesan level, impacting discernment to the priesthood for younger vocations.
- Passive recruitment efforts that have contributed to an aging clergy cohort.
- Past and current policies requiring life experience prior to seminary, thus delaying ordination.

- Availability of full-time parish ministry positions that can support a family or individual.
- Bivocational ministry options that meet millennial and Gen Z needs for sustainable work/life balance.
- Perceptions by Commissions on Ministry that chaplaincy is inferior to parish ministry and not really a call to the priesthood.
- Few options for discernment to ordained ministry for active-duty military and military academy students.
- Fewer funded curacies for chaplain candidates to develop Episcopal priestly identity and fulfill the federal government requirement of two-year, full-time professional practice prior to accession into the military.
- Perceived and real anti-military and military service bias in the church.
- Department of Defense policies on maximum age limits, and physical and mental fitness requirements for chaplain candidates.
- Clergy and seminarians interested in military chaplaincy unprepared or unable to meet the physical and emotional demands of military chaplaincy.
- Church-wide knowledge gaps on the role of military chaplaincy, and benefits to the wider church and the world.
- Knowledge gaps on military active duty and reserve options and benefits of military chaplaincy to the individual.

There are myriad reasons why vocations to the priesthood are declining, thus shrinking the pool of those that might be called to military chaplaincy. Long before parish or diocesan discernment processes start, robust youth formation programs that focus on Scripture, Christian faith and life, and engaged beloved community are important elements to prepare young people for a life of service and opportunities to plant the seeds of a future vocation. In conversation with young adults, stories of attendance at Episcopal camp and conference centers for retreats and programs as well as campus ministry that encouraged young people to form deep relationships with Christ and one another through acts of service, worship, prayer, and Scripture study were formative moments in the lives of those who eventually sought out ordained ministry. Leadership opportunities in college ministry that encourage deeper discipleship, transcendent worship, engaging the poor and marginalized, and *intentional* conversations around discernment to ordained ministry while young adults are still in college can offer the potential to affirm or even confirm the possibility of ordained life after graduation. This is especially important for students enrolled in colleges and universities that have a Reserve Officer Training Corps (ROTC), Corps of Cadet program as well as military academies. Students that make a commitment to serve their country while in college are often open to the possibility of a call to ordained ministry and military chaplaincy as well. These settings provide an opportunity for formation and time and space for the Holy Spirit to work in the hearts of young adults. Intentional recruiting by the wider church during these formative times in the life of young people has the potential of increasing vocations to the priesthood and military chaplaincy, and at present is under-resourced at all levels of church governance. For dioceses and the Episcopal Church at large, these programs require attention and funding if we want to attract candidates to the priesthood who are on fire for the gospel and desire reconciliation with God and the world. Young priest and seminary "first year" programs designed to help young adults discern a call to ordained ministry following graduation from college are also an excellent vehicle to encourage discernment towards ordained ministry and expose young adults to various ways one can live out ordained ministry in a parish, or in the case of military chaplaincy, beyond the walls of the parish.

With more and more parishes unable to support a full-time parish priest, bivocational ministry is a reality in many dioceses across the church. In parishes that cannot afford a full-time priest, military chaplaincy either full time or part time is a rewarding and viable option for living out one's call to the priesthood. Bivocational ministry can be a blessing if done well or bring about burnout in the life of an ordained person if it means two full-time jobs. Military chaplaincy in the reserve component of the various branches of the Armed Forces service provides a possible pathway for balanced bivocational ministry. It requires the cleric and parish leadership to set expectations as the laity take on more of the work of the church, especially regarding pastoral care and worship when a cleric is fulfilling their military responsibilities. Shared ministry can empower communities of faith to live creatively and use their gifts and talents to make a difference in the world. Additionally, the benefits available to reserve military chaplains can relieve some of the financial burdens that parishes face when employing a priest. Military reserve health benefit costs are significantly lower than some church medical plans, and periods of active duty may provide salary savings if worked out in a letter of agreement ahead of actual training.

There are many ways to live out the vocation of priest. Historically, the focus of ordained ministry has been at the local parish. This makes sense given the structure and canons of the Episcopal Church. However, this focus has created a perception among some Commissions on Ministry that priests and those discerning a call to ordained ministry in chaplaincy are choosing a lower order of ministry. As a result, in some dioceses military chaplaincy or chaplaincy of any kind is not discouraged but neither is it encouraged as an alternative option to live out ordained ministry in its fullness. Military chaplaincy is an opportunity to bring Christ to "the Front Lines of the Jesus Movement."[2] Military chaplaincy happens with and among the people of God in their workplaces, at physical training, on deployment, in combat, and during some of the most stressful times in the lives of the members of our military. This ministry also takes place on Sunday mornings at base chapel across the world where the diversity of God's people are on display as young people, military families, veterans, and retirees worship and celebrate Eucharist together. The connections made every day provide an opening for invitation to try on and be part of something many young adults have not ever experienced and that is a supportive and caring community of faith. Encouraging priests who have a heart for young adults and sharing Jesus's way of love through presence and care to consider military chaplaincy would benefit the world and the wider church.

Providing a vehicle for discernment to identify potential vocations for military chaplaincy among active-duty members of the military, particularly after they have finished their initial tour of required service, is an area of opportunity often overlooked. This would require coordination between the local diocese, parish priests near military installations, and Episcopal military chaplains to assist with discernment. Episcopalians serving on active duty if experiencing a call to the priesthood or military chaplaincy currently do not have a clear path outside of a diocesan process to discern a vocation to ordained ministry. Deployment schedules, military operations, and frequent transfers from duty station to duty station make it almost impossible to participate or even navigate a parish or diocesan discernment process. Creating a discernment path for ordained ministry for active-duty

2. Tillman, "On the 'Front Line.'"

military could encourage vocations to the priesthood as well as the diaconate and provide potential candidates for military chaplaincy. Additionally, with the advent of online and hybrid seminary programs, attendance at seminary is now possible for postulants serving on active duty.

There are basic requirements to be met before a military chaplain can be assessed as a reserve or active-duty chaplain. They are as follows:

- Education: Bachelor's degree greater than 120 semester hours with a 3.0+ GPA on a 4.0 scale.
- Must have a qualifying graduate degree greater than seventy-two semester hours; Master of Divinity preferred but MA in Theology acceptable. 3.4+ GPA on a 4.0 scale at an accredited seminary.
- Evidence of two years of full-time ministry experience post-graduation from seminary.
- Commissioned prior to the age of forty-two (waivers available depending on service need).
- US citizenship.
- Must meet all physical and fitness standards.
- Denominational endorsement.

All military chaplains are required to have two years of full-time professional practice to develop Episcopal priestly identity and fulfill the military requirement for professional practice or experience. These requirements are extremely important, particularly in a pluralistic environment where generic Protestant services are the norm at military base chapels and the skills of deep listening can make the difference between life and death. With the number of full-time parish positions decreasing in the Episcopal Church, especially curacies, it has become more difficult to meet this requirement for the newly ordained to develop the pastoral skills necessary to be effective chaplains. It will be important to identify alternative sources for funding full-time curacies to meet the requirement of two years of professional experience prior to accession. A private partnership that funds two-year, full-time curacies in exchange for enrollment in a military chaplain candidate program with a three-year reserve or active duty commitment similar to an ROTC program has the potential to encourage military chaplain vocations, assist smaller parishes that could use additional support to rebuild or develop, and train clergy for future ministry and leadership both inside and outside the church. It is also important to note that chaplaincy funding initiatives for curacies are vital to ensure the church's presence and voice in military chaplaincy. The spiritual care of LGBTQIA+ military and their family members is dependent on the availability of Episcopal and other progressive military chaplains who affirm their presence in the military.

One ongoing barrier to military chaplaincy vocations is the presence both perceived and real of anti-military sentiment and bias against military service within the Episcopal Church. During the Vietnam War, anger from anti-war sentiment spilled over from many churches and denominations including the Episcopal Church onto military men and women who were following orders to carry out the policies and wartime strategies of our government. Anger towards the war and disrespect directed at military members serving during those tumultuous years seriously traumatized our Vietnam-era veterans, and many still carry the wounds, scars, and moral injuries incurred during that time. Since the attacks of 9/11, however, there has been a renewed sense of patriotism, and whether for good or ill, especially with the rise of Christian nationalism, there has been a marked change in attitudes toward the military and military service. Churches that advertise they are military and veteran friendly not only affirm our military families and veterans, but they may also be places where future military chaplains feel safe to discern a call to military chaplaincy.

The vocation of military chaplaincy is as important today as it has ever been, especially in conveying the message of Jesus's love to the wider world. Military chaplains provide an alternative narrative and voice for peace as they advise senior military leaders whose decisions can lead our nation toward or away from peace. If there is a need for our military to support and defend the Constitution of the United States against all enemies, foreign and domestic, and sin is present in the world, the voice of military chaplains will be a source of support that can lead to reconciliation and healing for members of our nation's military. For those who choose military service as a pathway to a better life from places devastated by injustice and systemic racism, military chaplains play an important role in healing trauma and sharing God's love in ways that lead to hope and wholeness. Raising awareness of the justice work military chaplains undertake can also play a role in encouraging military chaplain vocations. There are opportunities for congregations and individuals across the church to raise awareness of military life and break down some of the stigmas associated with military service. Remembering military members in our prayers, honoring members of our congregations who have served our nation's military at appropriate times of the year, and supporting the needs of veterans and active-duty military members and their families in our communities are ways to demonstrate a positive relationship with the military and can serve as an encouragement for those experiencing a call to military chaplaincy.

The responsibility for raising vocations to military chaplaincy does not reside solely on the shoulders of the church. The Department of Defense has a significant role to play especially in regard to administrative policy and requirements surrounding chaplaincy. A life of military service is not for the faint of heart, and given the real physical demands of military service, a certain level of physical fitness is required. Shipboard life requires agility to climb ladders and strength to handle heavy equipment during fire drills and emergencies. In the field and combat environments, chaplains may need to hike long distances, carry a fifty-pound pack for ten or fifteen miles, or help move an injured service member overcoming physical obstacles to be present with those they serve. Carrying a fifty-pound pack while hiking ten or fifteen miles or helping to move an injured service member during combat would not be out of the question for military chaplains. Additionally, a military chaplain cannot be older than forty-two years of age at time of their initial enlistment. This originally had to do with the ability to collect a military pension before the mandatory retirement age of sixty-two. Since that retirement system has changed in recent years, a more liberal age waiver policy is in place given the shortage of clergy from liturgical traditions such as the Episcopal Church. Sadly, across all military services, it has been increasingly difficult to recruit young adults, including seminarians and younger clergy who meet the basic levels of physical fitness and weight standards. This has implications not only for military service but for the church as well. Rising medical costs for obesity-related diseases and illnesses are driving rising health insurance premiums. Programs and incentives that encourage healthy eating, regular exercise, physical and mental wellbeing, and counseling and support services at seminaries and through the Church Medical Trust are making inroads towards clergy wellness. By identifying these challenges earlier in the formation process, those seeking military chaplaincy will have information and time as well as the support they need to meet the physical requirements of military chaplaincy and service.

In recent years the number of eligible military chaplain candidates has been affected by the prevalence of young adults who are currently using prescription medications to treat anxiety, depression, ADHD, and other mental health issues. These medications are often a lifeline for those who suffer from mental health challenges, and while the military encourages those already serving who need mental healthcare to seek help, including medication, a medical waiver is necessary for those taking mental health-related prescriptions during their initial accession to active or reserve duty. It is not unusual for a potential candidate to be told to stop mental health medication for a year prior to accession if they are able.

Encouraging vocations to the priesthood and specifically to military chaplaincy requires intentionality, funding and raising awareness of the processes, timelines, and requirements for successful accession. There is a general lack of awareness throughout the Episcopal Church that the church even has military chaplains. This is often discovered at diocesan convention gatherings where there is an Armed Forces and United States Federal Ministries presence. Intentional and consistent communication to the wider church can make a difference and bring attention to military chaplaincy.

Military chaplains have many gifts to offer to the church during active service and when they return to diocesan or parish ministry. When not deployed, Episcopal active-duty military chaplains can be available to serve as supply priests, to support smaller congregations and offer respite to parish priests that might need a break or are on sabbatical. Some military chaplains do not have Sunday-morning military obligations if not assigned to a base chapel and unless in the field with their units are available to worship or serve at local parishes on Sunday mornings. Additionally, military chaplains have access to more young adults than almost anywhere else in the church. As such, they have unique perspectives on the spiritual needs of young adults and how the church can best disciple young adults given the challenges they face not only in the military but in life. Many of these young adults will never darken the doors of a church and our chaplains just might be a bridge to begin nurturing relationships between the military and churches surrounding our military installations.

When returning to parish ministry, military chaplains, especially those that are beyond their initial tour of duty, have extensive leadership, organizational, teaching, pastoral care, and deep listening skills, as well as experience working with spiritual "nones." Their knowledge could help the church grow both spiritually and numerically. Most chaplains are also team players and work well with others. This can make them a real asset in a multi-staff setting. Retired military chaplains also have health benefits that could allow a smaller parish to hire an affordable, experienced priest, and reserve military chaplains have access to reduced-rate health insurance as well. For these reasons, encouraging military chaplaincy as an option for living out a priestly vocation should be supported and encouraged by diocesan formation committees, Commissions on Ministry, and diocesan transition officers.

There are a variety of options for serving as a military chaplain in full-time and part-time capacities, and all have benefits as well as challenges. All military chaplains, whether full or part time, bring the gospel to the thousands they serve through incarnational ministry. Proselytizing is not allowed in the military as it can be viewed as coercive, but as a living witness to Christ, love and through worship, Scripture study, teaching, preaching, and living with and among our soldiers, sailors, airmen, guardians, marines, and coastguardsmen, Christ's love is made manifest by all that chaplains do in service to others. This is not without risk, especially during times of conflict, because even those that serve part time as reserve chaplains may be called to full-time duty. All chaplains will be in harm's way at one time or another during their career in the military. Given the nature of modern warfare, no longer is there such a thing as a frontline. Chaplains are expected and required to be with those they serve and that often means in places of extreme danger to life and limb. The potential to experience trauma and moral injury is very real and should not be minimized. Faith, hope, and trust in the living God that chaplains bring in times of conflict are paramount in ensuring service members are more resilient. The work of a chaplain can be compared to a healing balm that soothes and repairs the spiritual and emotional injuries that occur in times of conflict and war.

Military reserve and National Guard chaplains typically serve one weekend a month and two weeks each year. While this can be a burden to some parishes, it is also an opportunity to empower lay leadership in the parish. Letters of agreement that work out the details of a priest's absence from the parish and the responsibilities of the cleric and parish towards each other during these times will go a long way in ensuring a healthy relationship between both priest and parish. There is also another category of reserve chaplain called an Individual Mobilization Augmentee (IMA) who may or may not be part of a particular unit but works on special projects or supports a command for no more than twenty-four days a year. These chaplains can work for a few days at a time or fulfill their military commitment in two-week increments, balancing their military obligation with the needs of the parish during a particular season. They, like all reservists, have the potential to be called to involuntary active duty at any time, and all have access to some form of military healthcare benefits.

Some clergy regret not having the opportunity to serve as military chaplains earlier in their priesthood and believe it is too late as they no longer meet the age or physical requirements required by the Armed Forces. In some ways they are correct if they desire monetary compensation for their services. However, there are pathways for clergy in the Episcopal Church to wear a uniform, serve military communities, and use the skills they have developed throughout their lives to serve members of the military and military-adjacent communities in a volunteer capacity with the Coast Guard Auxiliary as an Auxiliary Support Chaplain (ASC) or as a Civil Air Patrol Chaplain (CAP).

The Coast Guard Auxiliary and Civil Air Patrol are two organizations that in time of war or serious conflict will serve as force multipliers for the United States Navy and Air Force by mobilizing civil air and marine assets in service of national defense. Coast Guard Auxiliary Chaplains currently serve on Coast Guard installations when a Navy Chaplain is not available to provide spiritual care or needs additional support. ASC chaplains are the only civilian clergy authorized to provide pastoral care aboard a marine vessel in the event of a serious accident. Often, they are called upon when units are returning from particularly difficult missions to provide care and accompany the crew home.

Civil Air Patrol (CAP) chaplains provide spiritual care to the more than 64,000 civilians of the CAP who assist with search-and-rescue efforts, provide comfort in times of disaster, and work to keep our nation safe. Additionally, CAP chaplains support CAP cadets and their families as they learn how to be leaders in their communities.

Since the founding of our nation, clergy have provided spiritual nourishment and care to members of our nation's Armed Forces, first as volunteers and then as military members living out their calling as clergy in service to and among those who choose to defend and protect the freedoms we enjoy as citizens of this country. Their service is characterized by courage, honor, duty, pride, loyalty, selflessness, commitment, faith, hope, and love, upholding the gospel as witness to Christ's reconciling love. Our military chaplains are some of the finest priests our church has to offer the world, and they serve as best they can wherever they are assigned. The vocation and ministry of military chaplaincy is unique, honorable, and distinctive, and will continue to be a gift to the church and the world for future generations, and this will require care and attention. May it be so.

Chaplains offer that change in vision. We may not be able to bring them anything new (remember contraband, nothing in, nothing out), we may not be able to take them anywhere, but we can change their outlook on their sentences and their own purpose for that time. We all need to bloom where we are planted, and if it is going to be rocky, sandy soil, so be it! Have you ever seen a desert flower? I have faith!

"You either do the time or the time does you."

BIBLIOGRAPHY

Tillman, Sharon. "On the 'Front Line' of the Jesus Movement." The Episcopal Church, July 11, 2018. https://www.episcopalchurch.org/federalministries/front-line-jesus-movement/.

www.ingramcontent.com/pod-product-compliance
Lightning Source LLC
LaVergne TN
LVHW020633100826
845148LV00012B/2164

* 9 7 9 8 3 8 5 2 5 8 2 3 9 *